The
Holistic
Gardener

Beauty Treatments from the Garden

Fiann Ó Nualláin

Illustrations by Sam Chelton

MERCIER PRESS

For Lisa – Is í an eorna nua tú a fheiceáil.

MERCIER PRESS

Cork

www.mercierpress.ie

First published in hardback in 2015. This edition first published in 2018.

© Text: Fiann Ó Nualláin, 2015

© Illustrations: Sam Chelton, 2015

ISBN: 978 1 78117 611 5

10 9 8 7 6 5 4 3 2 1

A CIP record for this title is available from the British Library

Printed and bound in the EU

CONTENTS

INDEXES

INTRODUCTION

This is the second in the series of Holistic Gardener books, each of which is aimed at promoting engagement with the array of beneficial plants we can easily grow in our back yard or front garden. The first in the series, *First Aid from the Garden*, was a huge success, hitting best-seller lists and selling fast. At signings and events for the book, I met many people with a genuine thirst for ways to remove chemicals and commercial products from their lives. This encouraged me to make beauty treatments the subject of this second Holistic Gardener book.

Being male, I did worry a little about tackling beauty, but nothing in this book is about conforming to current norms of beauty and attractiveness. I am not expressing personal prejudices or endorsing a societal ideal. Neither am I telling women (or men!) how they should look. I am simply exploring natural ways of maintaining the health of your skin, hair, eyes, etc., which can be considered beauty treatments for both women and men. Apart from things such as cleavage lotion or moustache wax, the treatments are pretty much unisex. To all I say, love your freckles, love your grey hair and, yes, protect your skin from harm and feel good about your smile. That said, if you can't love them completely, this book will help you at least care for them in a manner that won't harm you.

This book, like the first, is about adopting a somewhat self-sufficient and natural approach to health and beauty. There isn't a lot of that in the products marketed by the beauty industry. They use terms like botanical and herbal to create a halo effect, but why have ester of lavender when you can have real lavender? Why have a synthetic floral fragrance or a token extract of green tea when you can make a fresh hydrosol and a potent cuppa at home? It's not about thrift; it's about using the real thing. To my mind it is also about reducing the environmental impact of packaging and industrial pollution created by the beauty industry.

I have spent a lifetime studying and exploring medicinal botany, ethnobotany and holistic practices, so in this book I will borrow from herbalism, nutritional therapy, aromatherapy and even yoga, not just to banish blemishes, but also, hopefully, through the simplicity and beauty of a natural approach, to banish the anxiety of corporate, peer and societal pressure to be beautiful by purchase and be damaged in the process. As a gardener by profession and passion, this book was written with gardeners in mind, but the natural way is open and accessible to everyone, so just as gardeners share seeds and cuttings, I want to share the beauty of this approach to personal care with all.

WHAT IS NATURAL BEAUTY?

This book is about natural – rather than chemical – beauty treatments. It is about enhancing or revealing your natural beauty but also about the beauty that comes from nature – simple treatments from the garden, the hedgerow, the kitchen cupboard or the fridge. Many beauty products contain less-than-admirable ingredients, and the short-term fix must be weighed up against long-term health.

The history of cosmetic treatments is littered with dangerous practices. In ancient Rome women put toxic lead on their faces and during the Renaissance they used poisonous atropine to dilate their pupils. Today there are oestrogens, carcinogens and other nasties in manufactured products, which we can avoid by going natural. Many of the natural treatments I have discovered, and that I explore in this book, work better than commercial versions and can be had at a fraction of the cost. But natural beauty is about more than saving money – the reconnection with nature and natural methods may just save your health and even your sanity. As a holistic gardener, I know they will save your spirit and your soul and allow your natural radiance to shine through.

WHY GO NATURAL?

Gardeners are ecologically conscious. We face ethical choices head-on all the time: home compost versus peat, no-dig or manual methods versus chemical weed control, beneficial insects and biological control versus chemical pest control, the GM debate and so on. We inhabit a natural world, even if we attempt to manicure it and bend it to the constraints of garden design and personal taste. We are still in sympathy with, or at least participating in, nature. So if you bought this book as a gardener, you are probably already of a mind to live a more natural, chemical-free life and you will likely embrace the recipes as readily as you would a comfrey feed or a garlic spray. If this book was bought for you, it may be the first time you have considered the option of going natural over using manufactured products and electronic and chemical treatments. In that case *why go natural?* is a valid question.

I won't rehash the ethical debates, I won't plead with you to change your lifestyle, nor even push the mind-body-spirit aspect of embracing the natural. All I will say is read the labels on your shop-bought products, and if you see any of the following ingredients, you might want to think twice about sticking with the product.

ACETONE. Industrially manufactured acetone found in cosmetics is a solvent. It is also used to dissolve plastics, thin printing ink and as a paint remover. It is a skin irritant and is harmful to the eyes, nose, throat and lungs. Long-term or persistent exposure can shorten the menstrual cycle in women and cause kidney damage.

ALCOHOL is used in some natural beauty products to extract phytochemicals or to store them in tincture form. In commercial beauty products it is used to thin the consistency of a product and also to help other ingredients cross the skin barrier. In natural remedies the alcohol used is generally a natural grain alcohol such as that used in vodka, while commercial alcohols tend to be esters and/or chemically enhanced, often derivatives of propane or petrochemicals, such as isopropyl alcohol and ethyl alcohol. In general commercial chemical alcohols dry the skin, thin or erode the skin's natural barrier and affect regeneration mechanisms.

ARTIFICIAL COLOURS, often listed as E-numbers, feature in soaps, shampoos, bath products, hair gels, shave gels, toothpastes, body lotions, face creams, skin toners, face masks

8

and so on. Some colours are derivatives of coal tar and can contain heavy metal salts (including traces of arsenic and lead), others are synthesised using chemicals that can thin the skin and block pores.

BENZYL DIMETHYL STEARYL AMMONIUM CHLORIDE is used in lipstick, hair colourants, body lotions, shampoos and conditioners, as well as in some contraceptive formulations. Its industrial application is to boost the efficacy of detergents and industrial cleaners. It is a skin and eye irritant associated with occupational dermatitis.

BUTYLATED HYDROXYTOLUENE (BHT) is a toluene-based cosmetic preservative commonly used in shaving gels and many products aimed at men. Toluene is a toxic chemical linked to eye and lung irritation, hormone disruption and carcinogenic effects.

BUTYLENE GLYCOL is utilised as a solvent and viscosity-decreasing agent to thin products so they can be more easily applied. It can be found in concealer, foundation, moisturisers, sunscreens, eye creams and mascaras. When absorbed through skin or ingested, it is metabolised into gamma-hydroxybutyric acid, a depressant that slows down the activity of the brain and the central nervous system.

CARBAMIC ACID. See *iodopropynyl butylcarbamate.*

CARBOMER is a chemical made from acrylic acid or petroleum oil. It is found in sunscreen, moisturisers, shampoos and styling gel. It is a plastic and has all the endocrine-altering properties of plastics.

COAL TAR is a by-product of bituminous coal. It features in make-up and haircare products (dyes and anti-dandruff products) but also as a treatment for seborrhoea and psoriasis. Within the beauty industry it is considered a 'safe and effective' cosmetic biocide. However, coal tar is linked to phototoxicity, dermatitis and folliculitis. As a product of polycyclic aromatic hydrocarbons (PAHs) – a set of persistent organic pollutants – there are fears around the risks associated with its mutagenic potential and possible carcinogenic effects.

COCAMIDOPROPYL BETAINE features in body washes, liquid soaps, bath products, shampoos, toothpastes, contact lens solutions, make-up removers and other skincare products. It is a synthetic detergent that can lead to sensitisation and hypersensitisation. It was named allergen of the year in 2004 by the American Contact Dermatitis Society.

DIAZOLIDINYL UREA is a preservative used in cosmetics and toiletries. It releases formaldehyde and can increase skin sensitivity. Allergies and contact dermatitis are potential outcomes of exposure.

DIETHANOLAMINE (DEA) is often used in the processing of commercial soaps and shampoos, if it is not an actual ingredient. It is also used in industrial cleaners, pesticide sprays, agricultural chemicals and the rubber processing industry.

ESTERS are compounds formed from an alcohol and an organic acid. For the really scary ones, see *parabens*.

ETHYL ALCOHOL naturally occurs in wine, beer and other alcoholic beverages, but the commercial-/industrial-grade stuff is first denatured and then combined with toxic additives such as methanol (formulated from a combination of carbon monoxide and hydrogen), benzene (a known carcinogen) and paraffin (a petrochemical by-product). It can also be metabolised into acetone in the body.

ETHYLENE GLYCOL is used to make antifreeze, hydraulic brake fluids, solvents and plastics. It is derived from ethylene oxide, a primary ingredient of pesticides and insecticides.

FORMALDEHYDE is used in some cosmetics (particularly nail polish and nail polish remover) and hair-straightening products, as well as in plastics, building materials, carpet manufacturing, paints, industrial adhesives and pesticides. It is also used as an embalming fluid in mortuaries and as a disinfectant and preservative in medical laboratories. Prolonged exposure can cause asthma-like symptoms and increase cancer risk.

FRAGRANCE is not always extracted from flowers or fruit, even if it is floral or fruity in character. In the case of beauty products fragrance tends to be chemically composed, often using hydroxyisohexyl 3-cyclohexene, carboxaldehyde or isoeugenol. Artificial fragrances can cause anything from skin irritation, headaches and respiratory agitation, to long-term issues such as lung problems, hypersensitivity and dermatitis.

GLYCOL, GLYCOL ALCOHOL AND GLYCOL ETHERS are common in perfumes and aftershaves and are also contained in a whole array of beauty products and in industrial solvents and household cleaning products. They are commonly found in oven cleaners as they are powerful grease-cutting agents.

HYDROQUINONE is used in hair products and concealers as a colouring agent and a fragrance. With long-term exposure it is potentially carcinogenic, and in the shorter term it can sensitise the skin.

IMIDAZOLIDINYL is a preservative used in cosmetics and body-care products. It releases formaldehyde in the product and can increase skin sensitivity and lead to allergic reactions including contact dermatitis.

IODOPROPYNYL BUTYLCARBAMATE (IPBC) is a water-soluble preservative utilised in some face creams, body lotions, shampoos, conditioners, shaving creams and also in foundations, concealers, bronzers, eye shadows, mascaras, make-up removers, hair dyes and lip balms. IPBC is suspected of being a teratogen, which means it can increase the risk of birth defects and can lower fertility. In large doses and after prolonged exposure it is considered a gastrointestinal and liver toxin. In smaller doses it can be a skin irritant. It is sometimes listed as carbamic acid.

ISOPENTANE is a beauty-product solvent linked to dry skin and contact dermatitis as well as nose and throat irritation.

ISOPROPYL is a chemically manufactured alcohol produced through a process of combining water and propene by-products of oil refining via hydration reactions, or alternately by hydrogenating acetone. It is used as an industrial solvent, in windscreen de-icer and as a fuel additive. It is also used in the production of explosives and herbicides.

LANOLIN is found in lipsticks, hair products and many skin creams. It often features in so-called natural beauty recipes as it is obtained from sheep's wool, but it can cause contact dermatitis and skin sensitisation. It is poisonous if swallowed.

LEAD ACETATE is contained in hair products and in some cosmetics. It is lead! Do I need to say more? In case I do, lead is toxic, carcinogenic and damaging to the nervous system.

MONOETHANOLAMINE (MEA) features in shaving products and bathroom items that foam. It is linked to hormone disruption and the formation of cancer-causing nitrates and nitrosamines.

MINERAL OIL is obtained from petroleum by-products and can cause allergies and skin irritations in people who are sensitive to it. But even in non-sensitive people, it has a propensity to block pores and thus inhibit the natural elimination of skin and body toxins. The term *mineral oil* may indicate the presence of butylene glycol, propylene glycol, paraffin or even isopropyl alcohol.

NITROGENS, AS NITROSAMINES, are the carcinogenic compounds created by the reaction of two or more nitrogen-containing substances. If there is more than one *-amine* suffix on the list, it's likely a reaction has taken place.

PALMITIC ACID is used in many beauty products as an emulsifier. It has been linked with contact dermatitis.

PARABENS (notably isobutylparaben, butylparaben, methylparaben, propylparaben and parahydroxybenzoate) are used as a shelf-life extender in many cosmetic and toiletry products. The problem with parabens is their xenoestrogenic effect, meaning that they are shaped quite like oestrogen, and once absorbed into the body, they fill up receptors in your cells normally reserved for real oestrogen. The consequence of this is that other neurotransmitters and glands mistakenly start relaying messages and making adjustments based on the presence of what they assume is real oestrogen. Many modern foodstuffs also contain parabens to extend shelf-life. So, in terms of limiting your exposure, a home-made shaving oil or a natural moisturiser might be a good start.

PARAPHENYLENEDIAMINE (PPD) is present in many commercial hair dyes. It has been linked to allergic reactions and, after prolonged exposure, to skin irritation including dermatitis and hypersensitivity. PPD sensitising can have an impact on the effectiveness of some diabetic and blood-pressure medications (particularly sulfonamides and hydrochlorothiazides).

PARAFFIN (or paraffin oil) is a coal oil. This petroleum-based product is used as fuel or as a component of fuel, as a solvent for greases and also in insecticides.

PHTHALATES are considered obesogens. This means that they disrupt the normal hormonal activities of the body and trick it into storing fat. Any chemical that disrupts the endocrine system will impair immune function and many are on the radar for birth defects and cancer. Phthalates are contained in perfumes, nail polish and hair spray but also in body washes, soaps, shampoos and even moisturisers.

POLYVINYLPYRROLIDONE (PVP) COPOLYMER is used in the production of cosmetics such as foundation, lipsticks, etc. Allergies and dermatitis are potential side effects.

PROPYLENE GLYCOL is an emulsifying agent used in skin creams and body lotions. It is a petrochemical often used to smoothe skin, but can actually thin the skin and thus speed up the process and visible signs of ageing. It can cause contact dermatitis and short- and long-term surface irritations.

POLYTETRAFLUOROETHYLENE (PTFE) can be found in some shaving gels. It is the chemical agent used to make non-stick cookware, which has been linked with osteoarthritis, early-onset menopause and breast cancer.

SODIUM LAURYL SULPHATE (SLS) is found in a range of beauty products and toiletries on the shelf today. It is a foaming agent common in soaps, shampoos and body washes

15

but also in moisturisers, face cleansers, shaving creams and commercial post-shave balms. It can cause allergic reactions, eye irritation and, after longer-term exposure, it can produce a drying effect on skin and lead to other skin irritations. I worry because it increases the permeability of the skin and thus our susceptibility to other harmful agents in the same product or others used after it.

SODIUM POLYACRYLATE is a synthetic polymer from the crude oil industry, found in face masks, moisturisers, hand creams and sunscreens, as well as eye shadows and other cosmetics. The issue with petroleum products is that they can become contaminated or altered during processing, triggering interactions with other chemicals used in beauty regimes.

SULPHATES are potential triggers for dry skin and other irritations, including dermatitis. Product sulphates may also impair hair growth. They often appear in ingredients lists as sodium lauryl sulphate, sodium laureth sulphate or ammonium lauryl sulphate.

SYNTHETIC COLOURS are chemical in nature and as such may cause skin allergies and irritation.

TETRASODIUM EDTA (ethylenediaminetetraacetic acid) is a preservative made from formaldehyde, ethylenediamine and sodium cyanide. It is used in face creams, body moisturisers, shaving products, bath products, soaps, shampoos, hair conditioners and hair dyes, etc. It thins the skin's barrier, can dry the skin and is an eye irritant. It is sometimes also listed as a compound of edetate disodium, tetrasodium edetate, tetrasodium salt and TEA-EDTA.

TRIETHANOLAMINE (TEA) is an ingredient in products that foam, such as shaving gels and hair products. It is also contained in some cosmetics to balance the pH of the product. It can strip natural oils from the skin and hair and trigger allergic reactions in some people. It is a recognised eye irritant and is considered to have the potential to disrupt hormones. It is also associated with the formation of cancer-causing nitrates and nitrosamines.

UREA is sourced from mammalian urine. Yes, that's wee that's not your own. Often used as a penetration enhancer for products, it can cause reaction in sensitive skin and can sensitise other skin types.

VINYL ACETATE is found in mascara and eyeliner and also nail varnish. It is like all plastic in that it can potentially cause trouble with oestrogen receptors and can disrupt DNA.

XYLENE is a central-nervous-system depressant contained in nail varnish and nail varnish remover.

If you are still unconvinced, note that skin can absorb and deliver to the bloodstream around 60 per cent of any product it comes into contact with. In less than thirty seconds some of that make-up remover or hard heel softener is pumping through your heart, moving through your liver, arriving in your kidneys and piggybacking on the blood supply to your lungs and brain.

A WORD OF WARNING

A garden spa treatment is not necessarily suitable for every situation. Just as severe burns need medical attention and not a rub of aloe vera, so too certain skin conditions require the expertise of a dermatologist or medical professional. Also, not every remedy in this book will be appropriate for everybody. For example, people with an allergy to *Asteraceae* plants should avoid chrysanthemum or ox-eye daisy remedies, yet for everybody else they may be perfect choices. The seeds of hawthorn berries are stomach irritants and are toxic in large doses, but the fruit is edible and helps to build collagen. Understanding the plants and the parts you harvest for use is vital to adopting a natural approach to beauty. So, while I mention relevant facts, I also advise you to explore further or consult a herbalist to match your own health history to the information in this book (see *Ingredients and health status* below).

INGREDIENTS AND HEALTH STATUS

The treatments in this book are based on traditional recipes and on ones I use myself or share with friends, but they do not, or more to the point, cannot, take into account the variability of individuals with regard to sensitivities, plant allergies, underlying conditions, or prescription medications that may interact with a treatment. So if you are not sure of an ingredient or of your tolerance to it, I recommend you consult a qualified herbalist or naturopath. Otherwise all the usual rules apply: be cautious if you are pregnant, have blood-pressure issues or have a long-term illness or medical complaint.

INGREDIENTS AND ETHICAL CHOICES

To meet consumer expectations and achieve a commercial consistency/viscosity, I occasionally include ingredients such as petroleum jelly and Silcock's Base. As they are by-products of crude oil, some home crafters and ecological gardeners may have reservations about how those products impact upon oil reserves and the environment. On the other hand, most natural-cosmetics and herbal-medicine makers use them freely. If you have an issue, you can use zinc ointment, shea butter, cocoa butter or coconut oil instead. They feature only as carriers or thickeners, not as active components. In the instances of creams and lotions that call for emulsifying wax, its inclusion is vital to allow the oil and water elements to mix. Emulsifying waxes can be either vegetable based or petroleum based.

A GUIDE TO
HOME REMEDIES

Making home remedies is not only simple, it's also enjoyable. So fear not, this section will guide you through all you need to know about the processes and everything else required to get you started.

This book contains a dedicated recipe to address every listed complaint or condition, many laid out like cookbook recipes, which are simple to follow and execute. You can follow them without reference to this section, but within the *Garden spa* section of each complaint/condition I will often discuss the possibility of including other herbs or methods of benefit to that complaint. This section will help you explore those other options and also acts as a general reference where you can find basic versions of many of the recipes. I hope this will help you expand the healing potential of your garden and the herbs and medicinal plants you grow in it.

MEASUREMENTS AND METHODOLOGY

Most of the remedy recipes in this book are based on ratios, so as long as it's the same cup or same size tablespoon, no technical difficulties should arise. We may be making whipped body butter but we're not making soufflés! There is a margin for error built in. You can scale up to mugs and even buckets if you wish, but small fresh batches are best. There may be subtle differences in thickness or texture if you use a store-bought dried herb over a freshly harvested garden-grown herb, but the phytochemicals and benefit of the plant are contained in both.

This book is about an easy engagement with nature and natural health and beauty, so a sprig of rosemary in a cup of vinegar or a handful of leaves in a footbath will often do the trick without turning your kitchen or bedside table into a lab. Where a degree of precision is necessary to achieve the proportions that will effectively deliver the treatment or create a lotion and not a puddle, I give specific measurements in millilitres or grams. In the remedy methods I give a ratio or quantities that yield an amount of product roughly equivalent to what you would normally buy.

If you keep your salve in a warm handbag or backpack as opposed to a cool drawer or a bathroom cabinet, it may be runnier some days and suitably set other days. Similarly, if you stick with unadulterated emulsifying wax, raw shea butter, etc., the outcome will be different than if you add emulsifying cream and processed shea product. Variations are not a bad thing. There are no preservatives other than natural essential oils, alcohol, etc., so remember that shelf-lives are not infinite, which is no bad thing either.

So while this is all about handy treatments that are easily made and don't require a laboratory or any industrial processes, you should nevertheless consider preparation hygiene and sterile storage containers. The treatments are natural but they are still going on your skin or into your bloodstream, so avoid contaminating the natural goodness.

A NOTE ON THE CONSISTENCY OF HOME-MADE PRODUCTS

The recipes in this book were created to extract the healing potential from the ingredients, i.e. to be treatments, not carbon-copy versions of store or salon products. Where possible I have endeavoured to create a result not a million miles away from the bought product. But without the inclusion of chemical thickeners, preservatives and other agents that have no health value, the viscosity or texture of the cream or lotion may in some instances not match that of a conventional product, and sedimentation or separation can occur much sooner than with the commercial equivalent. You can shake the product before using, or whisk again, but by making small batches, treatment timetables of several days to several weeks will be possible. Castile soap, for example, is already thin and adding a herbal tisane to it to deliver a treatment will make it even runnier – something to pour over rather than lather in your hands. The really satisfying aspect of these remedies is how well they work as treatments.

WHAT YOU NEED TO GET STARTED

Key equipment
- baking tray
- blender
- chopping knife (chef's knife)
- cling film
- cooking thermometer
- cup

- double boiler (bain-marie)
- fridge
- garden secateurs
- garden trowel
- hob
- jam jars or mason/Kilner-type jars
- kettle
- measuring jug
- mixing bowl
- oven
- paring knife
- Pyrex bowl
- storage containers in various sizes
- tablespoon
- teaspoon
- timer or clock
- weighing scales
- whisk or hand blender
- wooden spoon

Key ingredients

- beeswax
- coconut oil
- coffee
- emulsifying wax
- essential oils
- kitchen oils (sunflower, olive, almond)
- lemon juice

- milk, cream and yoghurt
- plants from your garden
- salt
- soft fruits
- sugar
- water

HOW TO MAKE BASIC HOME REMEDIES

This how-to guide to making basic remedies will enable you to take advantage of your garden's healing potential by using medicinal plants in a variety of treatments and in a variety of ways.

The methods/recipes in this section are both the means of extracting the healing constituents of a plant and the means of delivering those constituents so that we benefit from them.

Some healing phytochemicals will quickly leach out of a plant into hot water (e.g. herbal teas and leaf infusions), while some will need to be boiled out (e.g. roots and twigs). Others may need an acid to extract the element we want, in which case we will use a safe acid such as vinegar or lemon juice. Sometimes an alcohol is required, and if an ingredient is fat-soluble, an oil or a fatty substance is called for. In many cases the method of extraction is dictated by the intended use. For example, a thyme tea is a great antiseptic rinse to treat dandruff, but a thyme salve (thyme infused in an oil base and then set with beeswax) is great for healing and sealing moisture into chapped lips or hands.

Similarly, using a different base can make an ingredient suitable for different applications. For example, calendula oil (the petals infused in some olive oil) can be used as a culinary aid to derive fat-soluble vitamins A and D from foods. Or it can be set with a vegetable or nut butter to make a replenishing skin cream. Or you can warm it to create a hot-oil hair-conditioning treatment that also helps psoriasis.

BALMS AND SALVES are made from vegetable or nut oil that can be herb-infused or not. The oil is heated and then set with grated beeswax or emulsifying wax. The distinction between balms and salves lies in the consistency and aroma – balms are often more fragrant and set harder.

How to make a basic balm or salve

In a bain-marie, melt 2 teaspoons of grated beeswax to every 3 tablespoons of sweet almond oil (or other carrier oil of your choice). Once the wax has dissolved in the oil you can add essential oil for fragrance or for its therapeutic value. Just one shake should be sufficient, but you can experiment to find the right amount for you. Stir the mixture well and then decant into small storage tins or jars. Allow to set at room temperature. Stores well for months in the pocket of overalls, the shed drawer or in your handbag.

BATH ADDITIVES. Some bath additives heal skin, some relax muscles and tissues, and some relax your mind or raise your spirits. There is a list of suggested additives on pages 231–35. Generally 1 cup of foliage or the same of liquid extract should be added to a full bath, but you can experiment to find the amount that's right for you.

BODY BUTTER. A whipped or more thickly set cream/lotion. Most body butters incorporate oil and water, so emulsifying wax is essential to combine these and for storage longevity. Here's a basic recipe to get you started:

How to make a basic body butter

In a bain-marie melt together 1 cup of coconut oil, 1 cup of shea butter and ½ cup of carrier oil of your choice (almond, olive, etc.). When everything has melted together, remove from the heat and allow to cool for 2 minutes before whisking with an electric or hand whisk until thickened to a creamy consistency. Allow to cool for a further 2 minutes and then whisk again. At this point you can chill in the fridge for 1 minute and whisk again. The chill often helps to develop a creamier, thicker butter. Decant into a clean storage container. This stores in the fridge or in a cool bathroom for three weeks.

BREW SHAMPOO is essentially a decoction of roots or aerial plant parts, often boiled up in a premade tea, tincture, vinegar or beer, rather than water.

How to make a basic brew shampoo

In a saucepan, bring to the boil 1 cup of liquid to every ½ cup of herbage. Turn off the heat and allow to cool. When fully cooled, strain to remove the solids. Then add 1 tablespoon of vegetable glycerine and 1 cup of liquid castile soap and stir well. Decant into a clean storage bottle.

CLEANSING MILK. Cow's and goat's milk are packed with cytokines (listed on expensive creams as peptides) that lift dead skin cells and repair tissue damage underneath while also stimulating the production of collagen and other connective tissues. When the healing quality of herbs is added, you get a potent treatment.

How to make a basic milk lotion

Quick lotions can be prepared by steeping plant parts in milk or by blending them with a hand blender. A good ratio is equal parts milk to herbage.

COMPRESSES AND POULTICES. Traditionally compresses are soaked dressings that can be used hot or cold. A piece of cloth (usually linen or muslin) is soaked in an infusion or decoction and applied to the affected area and held in place with bandages. But the practice of compressing has extended to pressing in place petals and herbage that have healing or cosmetic value.

Poultices are hot external applications of a prepared paste or pulp. They are made from the boiled fresh parts of a plant or from a paste of hot water and powder or the ground part of the healing plant and applied direct to the affected area. They are used to draw out impurities such as pus, stings, splinters, etc. The crushed parts of a plant can be applied cold as a poultice too. Certain petal poultices can have cosmetic as well as healing value.

CREAMS. Some of the creams in this book are made simply by soaking petals or foliage overnight in a dairy product such as buttermilk, yoghurt or cream, and are used as cleansing or toning creams. Other creams are more like commercial cosmetic creams and are made in a similar manner (but without preservatives and plasticisers). These creams are a blend of oil, water, emulsifying wax and herbs (if the herbs are not preinfused in the water or oil content).

How to make a basic cream

In a bain-marie, put ½ cup of infused oil and ½ cup of emulsifying wax grains. Melt and then stir to combine. Remove from the heat and pour in ½ cup of beneficial liquid (such as herbal tea, cold soya milk, etc.). Stir well and then refrigerate for 10 minutes. Remove from the fridge, stir well and then return to the fridge for a further 10 minutes. Stir well again until the mixture reaches your desired consistency. You can whip the mixture with an electric whisk at this stage if you prefer. It sets harder if stored in the fridge.

DECOCTION. This is a hot-water extraction of phytochemicals from plant parts. It involves actively boiling the plant parts for anything from 10 minutes to several hours. Several parts of a plant (twigs, roots, berries, leaves and flowers) and several plants can be used in a decoction, depending on the remedy recipe. For the most part decoctions are used to extract more phytochemical than would be possible by steeping in hot water. They are also used to extract from deep within the woody parts or roots of a plant.

How to make a basic decoction

The ratio of herb to liquid is usually 25–30g to 500–600ml. In a saucepan (avoid aluminium saucepans if possible) bring the ingredients to a boil and then simmer for 20 minutes. Strain and allow to cool. Only the strained liquid is used. Decoctions can be sweetened with a little brown sugar, molasses or honey to make a syrup. Decoctions and syrups can be refrigerated. Most decoctions will keep for three days, and syrups will keep for several weeks.

Decoctions can also be made by boiling in cider vinegar, beer or other liquids. A good tip is to crush, mash or score the plant parts just prior to boiling, to extract the maximum amount of the beneficial constituents. Foliage easily releases its volatile oils and other constituents to boiled water and so makes good tea/infusions, but roots and twigs often need to be boiled for quite a while. Many of the root and branch treatments in this book are decoctions.

ESSENTIAL TREATMENTS. In some recipes I prefix the titles with *essential.* This is to indicate the prominence of the essential-oil ingredient in the treatment. Essential oils are a distilled essence of a healing plant or its flower and are for external use only. Some essential oils have many contraindications, so you should consult a professional holistic practitioner or an expert book before using any oils.

Some essential oils can be applied neat to the skin but most must be diluted or blended with a carrier base to form a lotion or a cream for external application. Mostly, essential oils are blended with a cold-pressed carrier oil like sweet almond oil or grapeseed oil and massaged into the affected area or over the whole body during a therapeutic massage. In this book essential oils feature in salves and other recipes to boost healing value. They can also be used to add fragrance. See page 213 for a list of skin-friendly essential oils.

EXFOLIANTS not only slough off dead skin cells, but the action of applying them also boosts circulation to all layers of the skin, helping to eliminate toxins. This combination leaves skin supple and radiant.

How to make a basic exfoliant

The ratio is generally 1:1, i.e. equal parts wet ingredient to dry ingredient, be that 1 cup or 1 tablespoon. The wet agent can be a favourite oil, such as aloe vera gel or even fruit juice. Your dry ingredient may be leaf roughage, seeds, fruit rind or even kitchen items such as rice, salt or sugar. You can add extra wet or extra dry ingredient to create the consistency you prefer. See pages 226–230 for a list of exfoliant ingredients.

FACIAL STEAM. A technique to treat pores using boiling water and a herb or essential oil to create a medicated steam.

How to make a basic facial steam

The general rule is to add 1–2 tablespoons of herb or 1–2 shakes of essential oil to a basin and then pour over about 2 cups of boiling water. Using a towel to cover the back of your head, position yourself over the basin and let the towel enclose the basin and its steam, effectively creating a tent to trap the steam. Then just allow the herbal steam to open your pores and revitalise your sebaceous glands. Do not use steam if you have thread veins; instead make a wash of the ingredients to use at room temperature.

FUNCTIONAL FOODS are any edible or drinkable foodstuffs that deliver a medicinal or beneficial dose of vitamins or phytochemicals to remedy a condition. The basis of the *Kitchen spa* sections is to incorporate the therapeutic and nutritional benefit of everyday foods, some of which can be grown in the garden.

GELS. In some treatments the gel-like appearance comes from the sap of aloe vera or other plant extract with similar viscosity/consistency. This is just a case of mashing or pulping the plant part. In other treatments a gel is produced by adding vegetable gelatine as a setting agent to an infusion, heated tincture or decoction, just as you would when making a jelly. You will need to amend the ratios to suit the volume of the product, and there is a bit of trial and error involved in this one, as different brands/types of gelatine (leaf versus powder sachet versus a seaweed agent) can set differently.

HOT-OIL TREATMENTS. The term hot can be misleading as it is therapeutically warm rather than scalding. Many standard kitchen oils are easily infused with herbs beneficial to hair health. Simply warm to above room temperature or to a temperature you prefer. The heat facilitates quick and deep absorption. See page 63 for a list of oils suitable for hot-oil treatments.

HYDROSOLS are also referred to as floral waters. They are distillates produced from steaming plant materials. They are often considered an aromatic water and can be used in aromatherapy, but because they retain the essential oils of the plant parts, they have medicinal potential too.

How to make a hydrosol by steeping

Harvest some flowers and place the petals in a saucepan. Add just enough distilled/spring water to cover the petals, or no more than double the volume of the petals. Bring to a simmer. Cover and allow to steep until the petals lose their colour and it leaches into the water. Strain and decant into a container.

How to make a hydrosol by distillation

This method creates a pure distillate, similar to the witch hazel extract you can get from your pharmacy. Its concentration is stronger than that created by the steeping method. The process is more involved but it's worth it. Firstly, make your makeshift still; you'll need a large pot, a slightly smaller lid, a cup, a small bowl and a tallish

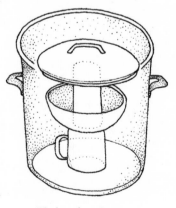

Hydrosol equipment

glass. Invert the cup in the centre of the pot. Then add petals to the pot and enough water to cover them, or no more than double the volume. Balance the bowl on top of the cup and place the tall glass in the bowl. Place the lid on top of the glass. The steam will hit the lid and form condensation, which will drip down the side of the glass into the gathering bowl. Bring the water to a simmer and keep it steaming, without allowing it to boil hard, for long enough to gather a decent amount of distilled essence. When the petals lose their colour you can stop distilling. If balancing lids, bowls, cups and glasses gives you a panicky feeling, you can use cling film as a lid (weighted down with a stone in the centre). It will funnel the drips into the gathering bowl.

INFUSED OILS. Infused oils are the basis of many recipes in this book. All flowering parts and foliage of both herbs and medicinal plants can be used to prepare an infused oil. Infused oils extend the seasonality (availability and storage) of the medicinal plants too.

How to make infused oil by heating

Using a bain-marie, heat the oil (olive, almond, sunflower, etc.) and add your herbs. The beneficial constituents will leach into the hot oil. For a more intense oil, you can simply fill a jam jar with herbs and oil and sit it in boiling water for an hour or so every day for several days, to draw out as much goodness as possible. This is a cheat's version of the sun-infused oil below.

How to make infused oil (sun method)

Simply fill a jam jar with as many plant parts (foliage, roots or petals) as will fit, cover completely with the oil and sit in a sunny window for a minimum of one to two weeks. This will allow the phytoconstituents of the herb to naturally leach into the oil.

INFUSIONS, TEAS AND TISANES. These are hot-water extractions of phytochemicals from plant parts, foliage and flowering tops. Hard stems, woodier parts or tougher roots are more often used in a decoction. Some infusions are drunk or sipped just like a herbal tea; others are cooled to form the basis of a recipe or are applied topically as a rinse, wash, spritz or compress.

How to make a basic infusion

In general 1 tablespoon of herbage to 1 cup of hot water is the ratio required. Extra herbage can be added for a stronger extraction. Simply boil a kettle, pour the boiled water over the plant parts and steep for 5–10 minutes. Sometimes extra steeping is necessary for a specific treatment and these are noted in individual recipes.

Teas are basically the same as infusions. Boiling water is added to a small amount of dried herb, fresh leaf or flower of a healing plant and allowed to infuse for 3–7 minutes. Then the solids are strained off, after which the tea can be drunk hot or cold. The ingredient ratios vary from remedy to remedy, but a normal amount would be 1 teaspoon to 1 cup of water. Many of the herbal teas mentioned in this book are also available commercially in tea bag form.

Tisanes are the mild form of both tea and infusion; they are not as strong and are not infused for as long. Tea made with a typical herbal tea bag would be considered a tisane; weaker than tea leaf but no less healing.

LOTIONS are similar to creams but are generally thinner. They are made using infused oil and a beneficial liquid (herbal tea, rose water, witch hazel, coconut milk, soya, etc.), combined, set and naturally preserved using emulsifying wax grains.

How to make a lotion

In a bain-marie, combine 1 cup of infused oil (strained of solids) and ½ cup of emulsifying wax grains. Heat until they are fully combined. Stir with a wooden chopstick. Remove from the heat and pour in ½ cup of water or similar quantity of enriched liquid such as cold chamomile tea, witch hazel extract or other herb infusion and stir well. Refrigerate for 10 minutes, remove and stir well. Return to the fridge for a further 10 minutes and then stir well again until you reach the desired consistency. You can whip the mixture with an electric whisk at this stage if you prefer.

MASKS. This book features hair masks, hand masks and face masks, all formulated to treat particular conditions or skin types. Some are a porridge mix (using oatmeal or flour with a wetting agent such as juice, water, milk, etc.), others use a fruit or vegetable pulp (packed with remedial phytochemicals) as a base. There is no standard recipe to follow; you simply mix wet and dry ingredients to achieve a consistency that works as a mask. In terms of skin applications the ideal consistency is not so runny that it drips off and not so dry that it crumbles. When it comes to hair, a runny consistency is less of an issue as you can wear a shower cap to keep it all in place.

MOISTURISERS. The primary function of a moisturiser is to create a barrier film upon your skin's surface in order to prevent moisture loss, but in doing so it also hydrates drying skin and protects skin cells from damage. The home-made moisturisers in this book also feed your skin some key nutrients. Any of the skin-tonic herbs can be made into a night cream, a body lotion or, for that extra-luxurious pampering, a body butter.

MUD MASKS AND CLAY FACE PACKS are made not from garden soil but alluvial clays with drawing/detoxifying and germicidal properties.

How to make a basic clay mask

Simply mix the clay powder and liquid to a paste. It is perhaps easier to sprinkle the powder into the liquid and build up from there. Once you reach the point where you think it's almost at the right consistency but a tad too runny, leave it to soak in for 5–10 minutes just to develop and settle. Finally, stir well and add more wet or dry ingredients if necessary. Wear for 20–30 minutes and then rinse off.

OIL LOTIONS/LINIMENTS. An oil lotion or a liniment is basically an infused oil used as a stimulating rub or a healing lubricant. There are two varieties: cold infused (flower and soft herb) and hot infused (spices, hard herbs such as rosemary and thyme, and also root and bark remedies).

How to make a basic liniment

To prepare a cold-infused liniment, simply allow the healing herb to infuse in olive oil for a period of five to seven weeks and then strain the oil through a muslin cloth. The ingredient ratio is usually 2 tablespoons of herb to 1 cup of oil.

To prepare 250ml of a hot-infused liniment, gather approximately 75g of the dried herb or spice required for the remedy (a higher quantity for fresh plant constituents) and place half of it in a heatproof container filled with 250ml of pure vegetable oil. Then place the container in a basin or bowl of hot water. Using direct heat or cooking the oil will diminish its healing properties, so we allow our infusion to heat gently in this warm bath for around 2 hours, adding boiling water occasionally to keep the bath warm.

After 2 hours the oil should have absorbed the healing properties of the herb or plant part and it will have altered in colour. Strain the oil from the herb/plant parts into a second container.

To this second container we now add the other half of our herb or plant parts. Place this container in the hot basin for a further 2 hours and repeat the heating process. Finally, we strain the oil a second time and decant into a storage container, ready for use.

PASTE. A quick topical treatment for acute symptoms. Some treatments call for a paste made from beneficial wet and dry ingredients, e.g. brewer's yeast and rose water, or petals mashed with tea or plant sap. The formula varies, but start with equal parts wet and dry ingredients and amend to suit your preferred consistency by adding more wet or dry as required.

POWDERS are simply the ground/powdered form of a dried plant part or parts. If you grind up dried ginger root it becomes ginger powder. Powders are used to introduce the healing property of the plant by sprinkling them on food, in cooking and by adding to beverages. Store-bought spices are considered powders. Powders are also used in the preparation of other remedies, such as poultices, or as a means of storing the herb for out-of-season use.

SCRUBS are exfoliants or tissue stimulators often made with store-cupboard essentials such as sugar, salt, pepper and coffee.

How to make a scrub

Simply mix 1 tablespoon each of carrier oil and scrub grains (sugar, salt, etc.) in the palm of your hand and, using your fingers, spread the scrub in circular motions over your skin. It exfoliates and moisturises simultaneously. Rinse off when finished and pat dry.

SERUM. An oil-based treatment for the hair or skin, usually combining coconut oil (for its thickening qualities) with an infused vegetable or nut oil. The basic recipe is 60 per cent infused oil to 40 per cent coconut oil, but you can amend the ratio to suit your preference.

SPRITZ. A liquid preparation (e.g. tea, tincture, decoction, etc.) applied using a spray bottle. This is as much a delivery method as a remedy, but the liquid base is also the device to extract the phytochemical from the herb – hot water will easily pull the antioxidants from tea, and so a refreshing green tea spritz can be used on the face, while the safe acetic acid of vinegar is necessary to pull the anti-inflammatory agents from woody rosemary or lavender. The bonus here is that vinegar is an anti-inflammatory in its own right, so a vinegar spritz is great for a rash or bruise. Make your spritz using the recipes for teas, tinctures, infusions or decoctions.

TINCTURE. A solution made by extracting plant constituents into an alcohol base. The resulting liquid is often referred to as a mother tincture. It can be diluted and taken orally or used neat as a topical rub or as an ingredient in other recipes. A tincture is as much a dosage as it is a preparation. It is usually 10–20 drops of a mother tincture diluted in a glass of mineral water.

How to make a mother tincture

The menstruum method is the traditional way to make a tincture. It involves soaking ½ cup of herbage in 500ml of vodka or brandy for four to five weeks. I prefer to use vodka as the more noticeable colour change acts as an indication of complete extraction.

The quicker method is to blitz the same ingredients in a blender. Then pour into jars, place on a sunny window ledge and shake daily for one week. Allow to stand for a second week and then strain away the solids and bottle up.

Dosage: Invariably 10–25 drops of the tincture three times daily for five days. Take a few days' break before beginning a second round of treatment.

VINEGAR RINSE. Vinegar is an anti-inflammatory and is also useful for safe acid-extraction of plant phytochemicals. You can add herbs to your kitchen vinegar to make medicinal washes and helpful treatments for specific complaints where the vinegar is as remedial as the herb infused in it. For example, in cleansing hair and scalp of residue, the vinegar also acts as a natural antimicrobial. Empty a bottle of vinegar, reserving the vinegar. Put as much herbage as will fit into the bottle and then pour the vinegar back in to fill the bottle. Allow to sit for two weeks and then use as required. There's no need to strain off the solids.

THE BEAUTY
TREATMENTS

HAIR AND
HAIR REMOVAL

HAIR

Shampoo commercials tell us that hair is made of many strands of a protein called keratin. In fact hair is more complex than that. It is actually a combination of two structures – the follicle, which is embedded in the scalp, and the hair strand, or shaft, which emerges from the scalp. The shaft is layered. Its innermost layer is called the medulla, and wrapped around that is the cortex – the moisture reservoir – which is protected by an outer layer called the cuticle. The cortex provides elasticity, integrity and strength and is responsible for both the colour and the texture of hair. Protecting the cuticle is a great way to maintain lustre and depth of colour. The natural shampoos and conditioners contained in this book will bolster rather than undermine that protective layer.

The hair follicle is the root of hair and is the truly living part. I address its care through the treatments and by selecting beneficial herbs to include in the shampoo and conditioner recipes. A single hair shaft has a normal life expectancy of two to six years. Then it separates from the follicle and falls away, to be replaced by a new hair shaft. This reminds us that scalp care is as important as maintenance of your mane. Many common hair problems arise from damage to the cuticle or issues with the scalp (e.g. sebum regulation or follicle distress).

46

Your hair is roughly 90 percent protein, and the remedies are formulated with this in mind. So while it may seem counter-intuitive to put dairy or food masks on your hair, these ingredients are often the best delivery method for the amino acids that make up those protein bonds. The phytochemicals in garden plants and common herbs can address many common hair issues too, so herbal rinses are a great way to boost health, body and shine. So much so, in fact, that the beauty industry is starting to appropriate the 'botanical' effect – for effect! But there's no mistaking the real thing when you make it yourself.

HAIR TYPES

The three main types addressed here are normal, dry and greasy. *Type* may give the impression that it is yours to keep forever, that it is fundamentally you. Not so; rather it is what is going on with you right now. You do not have dry or greasy hair for life. Some people will genetically have sebum-regulation issues that mean they lean towards a particular type, but for many, hormonal changes or environmental stresses (sun, air pollution, dye, styling treatments, etc.) have more to do with the condition of their hair.

NORMAL HAIR

For some, normal hair is an unattainable dream; for others it is an equilibrium found and lost repeatedly throughout their lives. If you're lucky enough to have it (or just curious about how to attain it) there are several things you can try.

Those with normal hair may have genetics on their side. For the most part it is a combination of good diet, a good haircare routine (no over-styling with products or heated equipment) and of course a balance of environmental/lifestyle factors too. Let's face it, it's hard to maintain normal hair with coastal salt spray or urban air pollution or spin class sweats or running your fingers through your hair in a traffic jam.

Garden spa

Beneficial phytonutrients for the maintenance of normal hair can be found in basil, parsley, rosemary, sage, calendula, chamomile, lavender, linden flowers, watercress, horsetail and nettle. All of these can be used in teas, but they are also great as cooled infusions in home-made shampoos or used at room temperature as a hair rinse.

Kitchen spa

Eating healthily will keep hair healthy. That means less salt, less sugar, less processed food and more fresh phytonutrient-rich vege-tables and antioxidant-rich fruits. The beta-carotene in carrots and sweet potatoes helps protect the skin of the scalp and also the health of the follicle and the pores that produce the natural oils that support your hair's defence and natural cleansing mechanisms.

Pamper day essential-oil soak

To a medium-sized bowl add ½ cup of geranium hydrosol (see page 35). Add ½ cup of apple cider vinegar and four shakes each of rosemary and sandalwood essential oils. Mix well before applying to hair. Can be allowed to dry naturally or used before shampooing and conditioning. Or you can add this to any of the hair masks in this book.

Basil, juniper and wheatgerm shampoo

Make a cup of basil tea (add ½ cup of chopped basil to ½ cup of boiled water, steep for 30 minutes and then strain off the solids). To a medium-sized bowl add the tea, 1 cup of liquid castile soap and stir in 2 tablespoons of wheatgerm oil and 4 shakes of essential oil of juniper. Decant into a clean container. Shake well before use.

Ylang ylang and geranium conditioner

Make ⅓ cup of geranium leaf tea (take a handful of chopped foliage, cover with boiling water and steep for 30 minutes). Put the tea in a blender with 1 tablespoon of vegetable glycerine, 3 tablespoons of natural yoghurt and 3 shakes of ylang ylang essential oil. Use as a 15–30-minute conditioning treatment and then rinse as normal.

DRY HAIR

Many factors can have an impact on the development of dry hair. Sometimes your scalp just does not naturally produce sufficient sebum to keep your hair hydrated. Sometimes your hair can't hold on to moisture due to environmental stress (sun exposure, drying winds, etc.). But mostly dry hair is caused by hair products, dyes and styling equipment that strip or 'heat out' the moisture/sebum or damage the cuticle that protects the hair strand and its ability to retain moisture.

Garden spa

Burdock root, calendula petals and comfrey leaves are excellent botanicals for dry-hair treatments, as are marshmallow root, rose, lavender, chamomile, geranium, elderflower, horsetail and nettle.

It is not so hard today to pick up jasmine oil or rose oil in your local grocery store; both will keep hair moisturised. Furthermore, both can be used in a treatment pomade, gel or conditioning oil with a little shea butter or a slice of garden-grown aloe vera or pulped *Sempervivum*.

Kitchen spa

Keeping hydrated internally is vital to preventing hair from dehydrating, so keep water or herbal teas to hand. Your body cannot produce its own supply of omega 3 and 6, both of which are beneficial to hair, so include pumpkin seeds, flaxseed/oil, nuts and plenty of dark-green vegetables in your diet. Also choose foods rich in vitamins A, E and K. Avocado contains all those vitamins and it can be used externally as a hair mask too. Simply pulp the flesh and rub it through your hair and scalp, leave it for 20 minutes and then rinse with a cooled green tea for extra shine.

Rose oil champo

What we know today as shampoo is actually Anglo-Indian for a technique rather than a product. It comes from the Hindi *champo*, meaning *to knead*. Treat yourself to a rose-infused oil hair soak to hydrate dry hair and promote scalp health. Just pour a glug into the palm of your hand and run it through your hair, massage your scalp and then comb through to distribute the oil to the ends and coat the cuticles. Alternatively you can use small amounts as a regular scalp rub. Remember that massaging will improve the blood flow to the scalp, bringing vital nutrients to the follicle and also stimulating sebum secretion, which will naturally help dry hair.

Honey, green tea and luxurious oil reconditioner

Honey is naturally absorbent and has been utilised as a hair reviver for thousands of years. Mix ⅓ cup of runny honey with 3 tablespoons of green tea and 3 tablespoons of your favourite infused oil (chamomile, calendula, basil, rose, or you can use one beneficial to your hair colour; see pages 67–75). The oil and honey mixture provides moisture, while the phytochemicals in the tea and the infused or extracted oils rejuvenate the scalp and follicles. Leave the conditioner in for at least 15 minutes. Rinse as normal.

Marshmallow, jasmine and rose shampoo

Put 1 cup of liquid castile soap into a medium-sized bowl and add 1 tablespoon of powdered marshmallow root (dry and grind your own or buy it from a health-food store) and 1 tablespoon of olive oil infused with marshmallow flowers. Stir in 1 cup of rose water (see page 143). Add 4 shakes of jasmine essential oil and decant into a clean storage bottle. Shake well before use.

Marshmallow flower

GREASY HAIR

Greasy generally refers to hair that is lank, flat or oily-looking. The hair shaft/strand sits in a follicle embedded in the scalp, situated at a sebaceous (oil) gland. The gland's secretions help hydrate the hair and also cleanse it by inhibiting the growth of micro-organisms on both the scalp and the hair shaft. In normal proportions sebum makes your hair shiny and healthy, but if it accumulates, it can make hair look less attractive and harder to style.

Sebum accumulation is not always caused by poor haircare. Hormonal changes during puberty or menopause can trigger higher sebum production, as can skin problems such as acne. Genetics can also play a part in supplying you with glands that like to secrete a lot. No matter the cause, the secret to finding a better balance lies in nutrition and also in the products you use and haircare regime you employ. Changing your diet or shampoo won't reverse genetics but it can help to regulate your sebum production, and for many that does the trick.

Greasy hair is sometimes considered to come in two different strains: one where the hair is greasy from roots to ends, with the presence of an oily scalp; the other with oily scalp and roots but with dry hair from beyond the roots to the ends. The shampoo and conditioner below are beneficial to both types, while the scalp rub is targeted at the latter.

Garden spa

Phytochemicals beneficial to an oily scalp and greasy hair can be found in bay leaves, burdock root, yarrow, chamomile, calendula, lemon balm, lavender, horsetail, peppermint, rosemary, sage, thyme and nettle. All of these are suitable for decoctions and infusions for hair rinses and also for pastes and lotions to treat the scalp. The astringent benefits of the extract of the bark, leaf or flower of witch hazel should not be overlooked either. Bergamot, geranium, juniper, cypress and eucalyptus can all be used to enhance decoctions, and in their essential-oil form too.

Witch hazel

Kitchen spa

Lemon juice and peel and also lemongrass can strip the oils from hair. Use sparingly so as not to damage the cuticle. It's best to use these in a shampoo or a conditioner to extract the full benefit while minimising the risk of damage. Apple cider vinegar is great to tone the scalp and remove some oil from hair strands. What you eat can help too: zinc-rich foods help to control sebum production, but note that zinc requires vitamin B6 (pyridoxine) for proper absorption. Both are found in oats. As well as vitamin B6, vitamin B2 is involved in regulating sebum production. Cereals are a good source of these vitamins, and if you switch to soya or non-dairy milk it can help to reduce the hormones that activate sebum. Read more about this in the section on greasy skin (see page 111).

Witch hazel extract

Traditionally witch hazel extract was obtained by steaming the twigs of the *hamamelis* shrub, but its leaves and flowers can also be used to extract gallic acid, kaempferol, quercetin, catechins, proanthocyanidins and eugenol, as well as the plant's tannin content. These are effective as tonics, anti-inflammatories, antiseptics and astringents.

Ingredients

- Water
- Witch hazel plant (*Hamamelis virginiana* and varieties)

Method

Gather some sprigs and twigs of witch hazel. They are more potent when flowering and just after flowering. Chop sprigs and twigs up into rough sections and then slice lengthways. Put the plant parts in a saucepan with a tight lid, cover with plenty of water and bring to a boil. Cover the saucepan and then simmer for a good 6 hours. You may need to add water occasionally if steam is escaping. Remove from the heat and allow to cool for 1 hour. Strain to remove the solids and decant the liquid into clean bottles or containers with tops. Pure extract will keep for one week at room temperature or several months if kept refrigerated.

Witch hazel extract can also be used as a skin toner, to soothe rashes and itching, to treat pimples, reduce eye bags and bruises and in treatments for varicose veins and haemorrhoids.

Tea tree and peppermint-infused apple cider scalp rub

Any vinegar (malt, wine or apple cider) will help remove dirt, mineral and product build-up from your hair, but apple cider vinegar is often less pungent and sometimes more potent. Adding a herb like peppermint and allowing it to infuse in the vinegar will boost cleansing potential and add extra phytochemicals to counter the greasy condition. The addition of 10 shakes of tea tree essential oil to every cup of infused vinegar will improve scalp circulation and cleanse follicles and sebum glands. The peppermint adds a pleasant vitality to the experience.

Tea Tree

Yarrow and lemon shampoo

Brew a strong cup of yarrow tea (steep the aerial parts for 20 minutes and then strain to remove the solids) and pour it into a medium-sized bowl. Squeeze in the juice of half a small lemon and add 1 cup of castile soap. Stir well. Decant into a clean storage bottle. Shake well before each application. Rinse well after shampooing.

Bay leaf and burdock root conditioner

In a blender, blitz ½ cup of apple cider vinegar, 3 tablespoons of castile soap, 1 tablespoon of vegetable glycerine, ½ cup of chopped burdock root and ⅓ cup of whole bay leaves. Massage in and leave for 25 minutes. Rinse with a cooled herbal tea that works with your hair colour (see page 67).

Burdock

HAIR PROBLEMS

UNRULY HAIR

Unruly is a term used to describe hair that cannot be easily styled, generally relating to frizziness or tangling but sometimes referring to coarse hair or extremely fine hair. Often such hair needs intense conditioning to nourish it, and oil or protein treatments to repair structural damage.

FRIZZY HAIR

There are several factors that can contribute to the development of frizzy hair, the weather being the prime culprit. Both summer humidity and dry winter air can easily cause frizz. Vigorous towel drying after shampooing can cause static, which leads to frizz too. Hairdryers and heated hairstyling equipment diminish hair's natural moisture, as do central heating and indoor environments. Commercial anti-frizz shampoos contain oils and proteins with the aim of coating individual hair strands and sealing the cuticle (outer layer of hair) against further damage.

FLY-AWAY HAIR

Those rogue strands are also often a result of heated indoor air, hairstyling equipment and other contributing factors mentioned above as causes of frizz. But for the most part fly-away hair is the result of static cling. A spritz of witch hazel extract can often solve this. It also helps to hydrate hair shafts and reduce excess sebum at the follicle.

Jasmine oil

Commercially available jasmine hair oil is simply a flower-infused oil. It can tame frizz and prevent fly-away hair. It protects hair from heat styling and the worst of the elements. It also helps scalp health and strengthens the roots of your hair. It is traditionally used to make hair stronger, less prone to static and breakage and generally more manageable, with the bonus of adding shine and fragrance too. To make a home-made jasmine-infused oil, simply infuse the flowers in oil for a week on a sunny window ledge, or chop the jasmine finely and add to hot oil 1 hour before treatment.

The biz overnight anti-frizz serum

Coconut oil is renowned in natural beauty for its ability to lubricate the hair shaft and replenish the cuticle. Mix 1 tablespoon of coconut oil with 1 tablespoon of jasmine-infused oil. Add 2 shakes of jasmine essential oil. Comb through and leave overnight. A shower cap will save the pillow. Rinse well in the morning.

The anti-frizz spritz

Add 2 shakes each of geranium, jasmine and rose essential oils to 100ml of witch hazel extract in a spray bottle. This will help knock the static out of fly-away hair and balance the hydration of frizzy hair. It smells so nice that even the bride of Frankenstein would get a second date.

BRITTLE HAIR

When the cuticle is damaged (generally by heat or harsh products but sometimes because of a vitamin deficiency, oxygen deprivation or natural ageing) the moisture from the cortex can evaporate, leaving a dried-out shaft prone to breakage because it lacks that subtle elasticity. All the natural treatments for unmanageable hair will help restore the elasticity and help seal the cortex. Eating foods that contain calcium, iron, zinc, copper and iodine can help to maintain cuticle health, but when it comes to your eating habits, do remember that a diet high in saturated fats and trans-fatty acids can inhibit oxygenation of the scalp and contribute to hair problems, including breakage.

Vitamin C fizzy shampoo

Vitamin C helps our bodies and the blood vessels in our scalps to process non-heme iron (the sort derived from vegetables) and also to form structural fibres, including hair. A crushed fizzy vitamin C tablet in 1 tablespoon of liquid castile soap and 2 tablespoons of green tea, massaged into the scalp and combed through your hair, will boost the vitality of your hair. Rinse with lukewarm water after 5–10 minutes.

TANGLES AND KNOTS

Sometimes this is down to not combing after activity that causes sweat and friction in the hair (such as a hike by the ocean, a gym workout or great sex). Other times it can be down to the water you wash and rinse your hair with. Hard water, the type with a lot of mineral deposits in it (you will know if your area is affected by how much limescale is on your kettle element), can dehydrate hair and diminish its elasticity, while also making it more prone to retaining dirt and product residue. Such hair will tangle easily and is hard to brush. Boiling water and letting it sit overnight can soften it. Sometimes mineral particles will float to the top or drop to the bottom, you can scoop those out, or siphon off the good stuff. Filter jugs are useful for this too.

Tangle-not conditioner

In a medium saucepan, put ⅓ cup of marshmallow root, ⅓ cup of soapwort and 2 cups of water. Cover and bring to the boil for 10 minutes. In a separate saucepan, warm together ⅓ cup each of olive oil, coconut oil and emulsifying wax. Strain the decoction to remove the solids, then whisk the oil and decoction together to get a lotion consistency. Use as a detangle soak and conditioning treatment.

DAMAGED HAIR

Hair is easily damaged by the heat of a hairdryer, the sun, the harsh chemicals in some products or even by the simple act of combing. Damaged hair looks dull, tangles easily, is difficult to style, becomes brittle and breaks. Many of the other treatments in this chapter will also benefit and nourish damaged hair. The treatments for frizzy or fly-away hair will repair hair too. In general, hot-oil and food masks tend to work best as dedicated treatments.

Garden spa

Phytochemicals that nourish the hair shaft, stimulate the follicle and encourage fresh growth and repair are found in comfrey leaf and root, burdock root, the foliage of lavender and rosemary, and the ever-helpful flowers of chamomile and calendula. Any of these, fresh or dried, can be infused in oil, brewed as a tea-rinse or used in a home conditioner, shampoo or vinegar rinse. A tablespoon or two of any of these will boost any hair mask.

Kitchen spa

Foods rich in vitamins A, C and E can accelerate the hair-repair process, as can those containing biotin, choline, pantothenic acid, inositol and zinc. But your kitchen can yield real treasure for damage limitation and nourishing repair. Why not make a hair mask from the healing foodstuffs in your fridge and pantry? The best ingredients for hair masks have traditionally been eggs, mayonnaise, banana, avocado, yoghurt and coconut milk. Apply a single serving or combine two to form a consistency that will coat your hair. Leave on for at least 10 minutes, then rinse and pat dry with a towel. Boost the treatment with a beer, apple cider vinegar or a herbal-tea rinse.

Hot-oil treatments for damaged hair

Many standard kitchen oils are easily infused with herbs beneficial to hair health. Simply warm to above room temperature or to a temperature you prefer (the term hot can be misleading, as it is more therapeutically warm than scalding). 15–30 minutes is a good timescale for a home treatment, but hot oils can be left in even after the 'heat' goes out, for a more intense treatment – for several hours or even overnight. Oils particularly good for damaged hair and suitable for hot-oil treatments include:

- avocado oil
- coconut oil
- sweet almond oil
- extra virgin olive oil

Quick-fix styling-heat damage mask

Apply a banana and coconut milk hair mask (mash the banana with a little milk to a mask consistency or purée to a lotion consistency). Rinse after 20 minutes with cooled jasmine tea/ infusion or beer.

Sun-damage mask

Make an aloe vera and avocado hair mask (in a mortar and pestle combine the fruit pulp and squeezed-out aloe sap) and leave on for at least 20 minutes. Rinse with chamomile tea for light hair and sage tea for darker hair.

Product-damage hair oil

Prepare a comfrey and hibiscus flower-infused hot-oil treatment (infuse the plant parts for a week on a sunny window ledge or finely chop the comfrey foliage and hibiscus flowers and add them to hot oil 1 hour before treatment). You can leave this in overnight (a shower cap will save the pillow), or wash it out with a shampoo suited to your hair colour. Rinse with lavender and green tea.

Comfrey

Post-dye hair treatment

Enjoy a 15-minute coconut hot-oil treatment (the oil can be infused with a herb that works with your hair colour: see individual hair colour entries). Rinse with beer or apple cider vinegar.

SPLIT ENDS/TRICHOPTILOSIS

Trichoptilosis, aka split ends, is a condition where the protective cuticle at the end of an individual hair strand is damaged, causing the hair to split into two or more strands. It is not self-limiting; there is no agent of repair other than triggering regeneration by trimming the hair above the point to which the damage extends.

Split ends are often a consequence of conventional haircare treatments – the heat from hairdryers, curling tongs and straighteners can damage the cuticle and cause splitting. Hair dyes can do similar damage. Some shampoos can strip hair of its protective oils and, with repeated use, can undermine hair health.

SOME HELPFUL HAIRSTYLING RECIPES

Flax hair gel

The word *flax* comes from the Old English *flæx*, via Indo-European roots that mean to plait or to twist, hinting at the plant's connection to linen/fibre, but the boiled-up seeds make a great gloop or gel that can stop hair twisting out of place. Simply boil 3 tablespoons of flaxseed in ¾ cup of water and allow to sit for 30 minutes before straining to remove the seeds. This keeps well in an airtight jar for several days. Flaxseed is often sold under the name linseed. (Never use linseed oil from a hardware store – it's treated for polishing furniture!)

Fragrant whipped pomade

Ingredients

- 3 tablespoons olive oil
- 2 tablespoons grated beeswax
- 2 tablespoons shea butter
- 2 tablespoons vegetable glycerine
- 5 shakes of your favourite fragrant essential oil

Method

In a bain-marie heat all the ingredients except for the essential oil. Once all the ingredients have melted together, remove from the heat. Add the essential oil. Allow to cool slightly and then whisk to a product-like consistency. Decant into a clean storage container. Allow to cool fully and set before use.

Quick-fix aloe hair gels

By directly applying puréed aloe vera, you can easily create a slicked-back look. It can be blended 50/50 with flax gloop too (see flax hair gel, p. 65) to achieve a strong hold. Or you can combine it in the same way with jojoba or jasmine oil for a conditioning wet look.

HAIR COLOUR AND DYED HAIR

Dyeing hair can strip the protective cuticle layer. It is important to condition before dyeing and in the days following dyeing. Hot oils infused with herbs suited to your hair colour will help seal the cuticle, protect the cortex and feed the follicle and shaft. Apart from the kitchen staples, try macadamia oil or argan oil to replenish hair and lessen the brittle-making effect of chemical dyes.

COLOUR RINSES

Whether your hair is dyed or natural, these rinses will enhance your colour.

Black. Rosemary and sage infusions are traditionally employed to bring out dark shades and black tea is used to deepen colour. Black tea is an astringent and can remove oil. Oil treatments in which the oil is infused with purple petals can add shine to black hair.

Brunette. Diluted apple cider vinegar can improve lustre, but to intensify colour, make a decoction of vinegar with rosemary, catnip, sage, raspberry leaves, walnuts, coffee or black tea.

Blond. Diluted lemon can brighten, but to enhance highlights and enrich tone, try rinsing with infusions of chamomile, calendula or mullein.

Red/titian. Black coffee is said to be a tonic for red hair, but to invigorate fiery tones, rinse with infusions of rosehip, calendula or red hibiscus.

Grey. An infusion of hollyhock or a decoction of betony can be used to remove the yellowness from grey hair.

BLACK HAIR

The presence of the pigment eumelanin creates black hair. It is a dominant genetic trait globally and is found in all ethnicities. Black hair naturally reflects more light, so it appears to shine more. The drawback is that you are expected to shine – it's a given – but environmental stress and harsh products can cause dullness. Hot-oil treatments and herbal conditioners will keep that lustre vibrant.

Garden spa

The phytochemicals in the following plants have an affinity with black hair: rosemary, sage, lilac, hyacinth, passionflower, lavender and veronica. Any non-toxic purple or near-black flowers can be used in infused oil for hot treatments.

Raven oil for dark hair

Sun-infuse sage and rosemary foliage, along with purple petals (from lilac flowers, cornflowers, hyacinths or violets, depending on the season and availability) in sesame oil for two weeks. Use as a conditioning oil to intensify natural tones and shine.

Cornflower

BRUNETTE/BROWN HAIR

If you have brown or brunette hair, you have the second most common colour on the planet. Your individual uniqueness apart, the eumelanin and pheomelanin balance aside, there are some things you can do to enhance your tone and sheen.

Having brown hair suggests that you naturally produce more skin-protecting eumelanin, and in general that indicates that you will have a more even skin tone. But as brown-haired people tend to have thicker hair than fair-haired people and less shine than black-haired people, it's all about the conditioning for you.

Garden spa

The phytochemicals in the following plants have an affinity with brunette hair: rosemary, raspberry leaves, catnip, sage, parsley, elderberries, nettle and beech leaves.

Brunette booster

For delicious chocolate tones try a 30-minute cocoa conditioner. Simply mix ¼ cup of cocoa powder and ½ cup of buttermilk (or kefir/natural yoghurt for a thicker consistency) with 1 tablespoon of apple cider vinegar and 1 tablespoon of glycerine or honey. Don't skip the vinegar, as it helps the pigment in the cocoa enter the hair shaft.

BLOND HAIR

Blond hair occurs because of a single mutation in a long gene sequence called KIT ligand (KITLG), a protein that binds to receptors throughout our body and affects not just pigmentation but blood and nerve cells and even sex cells – maybe blonds do have more fun! 'They do with me,' should always be your answer! But the cultural sexualisation of blonds is a spillover from sexual selection, where blond hair is perceived as a point of excitement by males who seem to connect the 'youth' of blondness with fertility and playfulness (sexual receptiveness). The truth is perhaps more about evolution and natural selection; depigmentation during the last Ice Age allowed more effective absorption of ultraviolet B (UVB), which is essential to synthesising the previtamin D3 and therefore to maintaining healthy functioning of the body. Blonds were 'fitter' back then in at least one sense of the word!

Garden spa

The phytochemicals in the following plants have an affinity with blond hair: chamomile, evening primrose, yellow primrose, mullein, purple loosestrife, horsetail and nettle.

Blond brightening blitz mask

There are enzymes in raw potato that naturally lighten blond hair and if mixed with the lightening chemicals in chamomile and the soft bleaching acids in lemon juice can brighten your locks a few extra shades.

Method

Simply slice 1 lemon and blitz the slices (juice, flesh and rind) with 1 grated, raw, peeled potato and 2 tablespoons of chamomile flowers. You can add some chamomile tea or extra water if the consistency is too thick. Use as a 20-minute treatment mask. This keeps in the fridge for three days if you need to repeat the treatment.

RED HAIR

Red hair is all down to the pigment called pheomelanin, which also imparts colour to the lips. The interesting thing is that the intensity of the pigment in redheads is caused by a recessive genetic trait (inherited from both parents) that alters the melanocortin 1 receptor (MC1R) gene, so it not only colours the hair but causes lower melanin levels in the skin, making it paler. Lighter skin absorbs more sunlight, which is great for the production of vitamin D but means a higher risk of sunburn (see page 149). Pheomelanin also increases the likelihood of freckles (see page 144).

The issue with natural redheads is that pheomelanin degrades in the presence of UV light, so summer bleaching can occur. The same issue relates to reds from a bottle – red dye pigments are also UV sensitive. So avoid the midday sun and consider adding a few hats and headscarves to your wardrobe. Natural red tends to be slightly dry, and hair that is dyed red is essentially stripped of its oils, so regular hot-oil treatments will keep fiery locks aflame.

Garden spa

Infuse oil with orange or red petals to strengthen colour tone. The oil moisturises and protects against UV damage.

Kitchen spa

Using conditioning soaks containing cranberry juice and other red juices (if using beetroot juice, dilute it, as it can stain the scalp) is a way to rejuvenate colour tone while at the same time moisturising. The vitamin A in a carrot juice rinse will enrich lustre.

Calendula

Ginger, hibiscus and calendula shampoo

The inclusion of ginger in a shampoo for red hair is only slightly tongue in cheek. Ginger is good, and real ginger is great. It will stimulate circulation in the scalp; that tingle it imparts is caused by the oxygenation of follicles. Calendula is a good pigment for red hair and is also nutritious for dry and UV-sensitive hair.

Ingredients

- 2 tablespoons grated ginger root
- ½ cup calendula petals
- 1 cup hibiscus tea
- 1 cup liquid castile soap

Method

Boil the ginger and petals in the hibiscus tea for 20 minutes and then allow to cool completely. Strain to remove the solids. Add the liquid soap and stir. Decant into a clean storage bottle. Shake well before each use. Use as a pour-over shampoo. Refrigerates for up to two weeks, but you will use it all long before that.

GREY HAIR AND GREYING HAIR

The colour in hair is due to a pigment called melanin, which is produced by hair follicles. As we age, our follicles slow their production of melanin and the colour begins to lose its intensity and eventually fades to grey. Hair usually begins to grey at the temples and then moves towards the top of the scalp. Body and facial hair may also turn grey but later and at a slower rate than the hair on your head. Underarm and pubic hair may grey less or even not at all. Greying can begin as early as your twenties.

Greying is a natural process and is beautiful in its own right. There is no magic bullet to stop it and I am not so sure if science needs a 'cure' for it. The cosmetics industry makes a fortune from convincing people to cover it up. I feel that just as stepping away from seasonal foods to processed convenience food has undermined health, so too trying to avoid ageing may be detrimental. Nature has a rhythm and it's good to dance in time with it. But if you're determined to slow down the greying process, you can try the ideas below.

Garden spa

You can always grow and eat plenty of garlic, onions and cruciferous vegetables (cabbage, kale, broccoli, etc.), which contain the super antioxidant catalase. But a great way to de-stress and slow the ravages of ageing is to get grounded; take a little time out and walk barefoot on your lawn. Walking barefoot on the earth (your lawn, the beach, the turned-over veg patch) is possibly the most effective way of neutralising free-radical damage. The earth (planet Earth's surface) contains an infinite number of free electrons that are natural antioxidants and cell rejuvenators. Grounding increases the ability of catalase to do its job. See *The benefits of barefoot gardening* on page 263 for more.

Kitchen spa

Coconut oil contains catalase. A pomade made with coconut oil will not reverse greying but it can slow it down. Likewise eating foods rich in catalase and its precursors can help slow progression. Avocado, apples, cherries and melons are high in catalase, as are leafy veg, barley, wheat and sprouts. Cooking can kill off the enzyme, so eat them raw or in smoothies. Also, it is a good idea to not eat them as part of a meal but rather one at a time, and wait an hour before eating anything else. This gives the best chance for absorption to take place because it stops too much stomach acid from destroying the enzyme.

Avocado

OTHER HAIR PROBLEMS

LACKLUSTRE HAIR

Environmental stresses and some styling products can deplete your natural oils and the healthy sheen from your hair. Commercial shampoos, if not thoroughly rinsed, can also leave hair dull. Infusing kitchen oils with garden herbs can create sheen-boosting hot-oil treatments, and herbal-tea infusions make great rinses and are also brilliant bases for shampoos and conditioning treatments that put some shine back. A flat-beer spritz is also a beneficial, if subtly aromatic, treatment (simply stir the carbonation out before decanting into a sprayer).

LIMP, LIFELESS HAIR

This is most often a problem with fine hair, but all hair types are susceptible. The trick is to boost hair health with nutrition and manage hair condition on a weekly basis. One quick solution is to volumise your hair with natural products such as Epsom salts, citrus juice, apple cider vinegar, beer and even sugar, which can be brushed through in small quantities. Too much sebum or even added hair oil can also make hair limp. Use astringent witch hazel extract as the basis for your home-made shampoos and rinses. Rosemary not only wakes up the follicles but also degreases, cleanses and revives hair strands.

RESIDUE-RIDDEN HAIR

Using too much product often contributes to both of the above problems, but it can be an issue in its own right. A pinch of brewer's yeast added to ½ cup of beer will remove residue and revitalise hair. A peppermint and sodium-bicarbonate rinse (2 tablespoons of baking soda added to ½ cup of peppermint tea) can strip excess product while also pepping up follicles. Massage through hair and scalp, leave for 3 minutes and rinse thoroughly with lukewarm water.

Garden spa

Make your own scalp and hair tonics using witch hazel extract (see page 55), rosemary vinegar, calendula oil or jasmine oil (see page 59). Grow and harvest hops for volume-boosting hair rinses or save back some of the beer you pour for slugs to make a beer shampoo.

Kitchen spa

Yeast plumps up volume; try a beer rinse or add brewer's yeast to a conditioner. The lactic acid in milk, cream and yoghurt helps strip away dirt and grime from hair in a gentle manner, but the real bonus lies in the fact that dairy fats will moisturise and replenish hair. Some swear by egg masks and certainly the yolk of an egg, while naturally moisturising, is quite rich in volume-boosting fats and replenishing proteins. Egg whites contain enzymes that can remove excess oils, which is great for limpness caused by greasiness/sebum.

Nettle and rosemary beer brew shampoo

In a medium saucepan, bring to the boil 1 cup of beer, ½ cup of chopped nettles and 1 sprig of rosemary. Then turn off the heat and allow to cool. When fully cooled, remove the rosemary sprig and strain to remove the nettle solids. Add 1 tablespoon of vegetable glycerine and 1 cup of liquid castile soap. Stir well and decant into a clean storage bottle.

Greek yoghurt hair soak

Yoghurt is packed with vitamin D, which supports follicle health. It also contains lots of vitamin B5, a hair-friendly protein you may recognise (often plastered on the side of commercial conditioners) as pantothenic acid. Use unadulterated yoghurt as a hair mask/20-minute leave-in conditioner. Rinse off with water or a cooled herbal infusion that works with your hair colour.

Rosemary

DANDRUFF

Beyond itchy irritation, dandruff is an embarrassing nuisance, leaving white flakes of skin in your wake, or at least all over your shoulders. There is also a false belief that it indicates poor hygiene. In reality dandruff isn't about how often you wash your hair; it is more about the health of your scalp. Dandruff is the result of Pityrosporum ovale or Pityriasis simplex capillitii, which are fungi that cause skin cells to grow too fast and die off just as quick, hence the shedding.

Garden spa

Herbs such as rosemary, sage and lavender, or plants such as nettle and horsetail, can make great rinses to improve circulation and nutrition to the scalp. Garden-grown thyme, which is a natural antimicrobial (often employed for stubborn fungal infections in other parts of the body), can help combat both scalp fungus and also the dandruff flakes, including those related to seborrheic dermatitis. Other plants that help the condition include calendula, chamomile, rose, hyssop, peony, field scabious and catmint, while many old herbal treatments use comfrey leaf, burdock root and also marshmallow root. Any of the mint varieties – pepper, spear or common – will cool the scalp and can be used in an infused oil, a tea rinse, a vinegar rinse or even in a paste of leaves blitzed with coconut oil.

Kitchen spa

Apple cider vinegar diluted 50/50 with water makes a great anti-inflammatory scalp cleanser as a 20-minute soak or quick rinse. Boost it by infusing it with any of the herbs and plants mentioned above.

Essential dandruff remedy

Make a simple scalp rinse by combining tea tree essential oil and witch hazel extract. This pits two potent antimicrobial and astringent agents against the dandruff fungus. The great thing about this treatment is that the solution also softens and disrupts the integrity of the fungal membrane, breaking down the scaly barrier that acts as a defence against our natural immune response. This allows our immune system to penetrate the fungal membrane. When we repeatedly enable better penetration, this trains our immune system how and where to tackle repeat incursions by the *Pityrosporum* fungus.

Burdock root brew shampoo

Burdock root is both astringent and antibacterial but it also contains properties that alleviate skin irritation and scalp itchiness. To a medium saucepan add ½ cup of chopped burdock root to 1 cup of beer. Bring to the boil. Reduce the heat and simmer with the lid on to decoct for 30 minutes. Allow to cool naturally and then strain to remove the solids. Add 1 cup of fragrance-free liquid soap or non-allergenic baby shampoo. Decant into a clean storage bottle and use as you would a regular shampoo.

Nettle and cider vinegar conditioner

A nettle infusion will condition both hair and scalp and help to treat dandruff, but you can make a stronger version by decocting the nettles in apple cider vinegar for 20 minutes, cooling and then blitzing in the blender with 1 tablespoon of honey and 1 tablespoon of glycerine. Leave in for 20–30 minutes. Rinse with warm water.

THINNING HAIR AND HAIR LOSS

Shedding hair is as natural a process as growing hair; in fact it is part of it. It is completely normal to shed 50–100 hairs every day as part of the growth cycle, the first phase of which is called anagen, when hair grows out of the follicle bed at a rate of approximately 1cm per month for roughly three months. Then it becomes dormant for another three-month phase (referred to as telogen). Following this a second anagen phase occurs, generating a new hair shaft that is active for the next three months and eventually dislodges the old dormant strand.

It becomes a thinning issue when stress, mechanical manipulation (plucking and also harsh treatments and styling), hormonal activity or natural ageing undermine the follicles' ability to produce sturdy hair shafts. Then the hair becomes finer (thinner in appearance) or is more prone to damage, breakage and shedding.

Hormone-related hair loss. Androgens (often called male hormones but present in lower quantities in women) have a role in regulating hair growth. An overproduction of androgens can cause the hair follicle to gradually become smaller (miniaturisation), triggering finer hairs to emerge, thus thinning. This can progress to pattern baldness. Androgens can surge in women during menopause. For men the particular androgen involved is dihydrotestosterone (DHT), which effectively triggers early shedding.

Hair loss triggered by vitamin deficiency. An unbalanced diet can trigger deficiencies in the follicle and lead to temporary hair loss. Hair manufacture and growth requires biotin, niacin, B6, B12, zinc and vitamins A and E.

Hair loss due to poor haircare regime. Allowing your hair to become dehydrated over prolonged periods through stress caused by chemical products or environmental factors can lead to breakage close to the roots, causing thinning to occur.

Medicine and thinning. Some medicines, and in particular cancer treatments, can thin hair or make it fall out altogether. Consult your GP if thinning follows on foot of a new medicine you have been prescribed. Post-chemotherapy, hair will naturally grow back.

Garden spa

Rosemary, basil, sage and nettle have long been used to stave off hair loss/thinning, both through internal and external applications. Ginger, peppermint, mint, lemon balm and other stimulating herbs have a place as hair tonics and follicle detoxifiers. Arnica may also help to encourage hair generation.

Kitchen spa

Biotin is perhaps the most important B vitamin when it comes to hair growth and follicle health. Deficiency is rare as we make our own biotin in our intestines and it is plentiful in eggs, almonds, walnuts, peanuts, avocados, raspberries and lots of common foods, many of which can be used in a hair mask or be puréed into a treatment conditioner.

A percolated rinse

Commercial shampoos containing caffeine are promoted on the basis that they energise hair roots and make them stronger. The same action, perhaps intensified, is achievable by rinsing your hair with a strong cup of cooled black coffee.

FACIAL HAIRCARE AND MAINTENANCE

FACIAL HAIR DOS AND DON'TS

Shampooing with standard shampoos or soap can dry the skin underneath facial hair and residual product can damage the cuticles of the hair. Coconut oil used raw as a moisturising conditioner will hydrate the skin and the roots and tips of beards, sideburns and moustaches. The heat of your hands will melt the coconut oil, so it's easy to apply.

Houseleek

Wiry beard

The sap of houseleek or aloe vera can soften wiry beards and benefit any inflamed or scaly skin underneath. Similarly, coconut oil is also a treatment for both beard hair and the skin beneath.

Itchy, flaky beard or moustache

Extracts of rosemary, thyme, calendula, yarrow and witch hazel can all reduce itchiness and flakiness. Infuse all of the above (or whatever you have to hand) in an apple cider vinegar base or in apple cider and use as a leave-in conditioner and skin treatment. Add B5 (pantothenic acid) by stirring 1 tablespoon of ground sunflower seeds into some natural yoghurt and using as a 20-minute conditioning treatment.

Beard and moustache shampoo

Purée 3 tablespoons of liquid soap with 1 tablespoon of aloe vera gel/sap, 1 tablespoon of coconut oil and 1 teaspoon of glycerine. Lather up with a little green tea.

Beard and moustache shampoo to strip oil and residual product

Soften a lime in a little boiling water. Halve, deseed and blitz it in a blender (peel included) with 2 tablespoons of sunflower oil and 4 tablespoons of castile liquid soap.

Beard and moustache conditioner

The silicon and sulphur in cucumbers stimulate hair growth. Chop and then blitz a cucumber in the blender and apply as a 30-minute leave-in treatment.

Moustache wax

Put 1 tablespoon of wheatgerm oil and 25g each of coconut oil and grated beeswax in a bain-marie. Heat until the ingredients are melted and stir to combine. Cool until the mixture is set. This makes a conditioning wax that can help to style a moustache, but the heat of your face and your skin's natural absorbency mean the style might not last very long. If you are going for a full-on Salvador Dali look, a hair-setting product is required. Try commercial hard soap, firm-hold gel, or if you want something natural, a setting gloop of flax hair gel (see page 65).

HAIR REMOVAL

Just like a weed, sometimes a hair is simply in the wrong place, be it sprouting from your chin, your nasal passage or your ear. Then there are parts of the body that contemporary society has decided should be hairless. Cosmetically there are two general hair-removal methods – depilation and epilation – each with variations but all of which are temporary solutions.

Depilation is the removal of hair above the surface of the skin either by shaving or by trimming back. Its effect can last anywhere from several hours to several days. It also lends its name to depilatory products – creams or powders that chemically dissolve the protein bonds of surface hair.

Epilation is the removal of the entire hair from the follicle by waxing or plucking, creating a result that lasts anything from several days to several weeks. Methods include threading, sugaring, mechanised methods using devices such as epilators, which extract hairs from the root, and laser treatments too.

Whether or not more-permanent hair removal is possible depends on the hair type of the individual and the location of the hair to be removed. Electrolysis and laser treatment are not suited to every hair type. You should discuss these treatments with your dermatologist or beautician.

SHAVING

Shaving is perhaps the quickest and easiest method of hair removal. It is not suitable for every situation or location, but it works. Archaeological evidence suggests we've been doing it since the spear and wheel were invented!

Shaving tips for a closer shave. Commercial shaving foams can dry out the skin, while gels are somewhat less irritating. Home shave oils or gels are formulated to suit your needs and can contain anti-reddening, anti-inflammatory or antibacterial herbs. The point of using foam or lubricants is not so much to create a smooth glide (which is helpful of course) but rather that lubricated hair is easier to shave and less likely to become ingrown. Before shaving, wash your face, legs or other areas to exfoliate dead cells and lift the hairs to allow for a closer shave.

Shaving tips to prevent ingrown hairs and razor bumps. Again, wash the skin and allow it to lubricate for 3–5 minutes with a shaving agent or water. This will lift and plump up the hair shafts. You should also shave in the right direction. For the face and legs this means shaving downward, and for the neck the direction is upwards. For other areas go with the direction of the growth. Stretching the skin too taut or repeated shaving of the same area will result in the hair being cut too short and potentially cause it to grow inwardly. This can also cause the follicle to become irritated.

SHAVING SUPPORTS

Pre-shave exfoliator

This helps to make a closer shave possible by removing dead skin cells and plumping up the hairs to be removed. A simple scrub can be made with 1 spoon each of glycerine, liquid soap and witch hazel and ½ spoon of nigella or poppy seeds. Whether you use teaspoons or tablespoons depends on the size of the area you want to exfoliate. Rinse well. (See also *Natural exfoliants* on page 226).

Men's shaving oil

To 50ml of vegetable or nut oil add 30ml of fragrance-free liquid soap, 1 tablespoon of glycerine, 5 shakes of cedar wood essential oil and 5 shakes of juniper essential oil. Or if you prefer a different fragrance, try anti-inflammatory tea tree, thyme, fennel, clove or oregano. Decant into a storage bottle. Stir or shake well before use. Stores for several months in your bathroom cabinet.

Women's shaving oil

To 50ml of soybean oil add 30ml of fragrance-free liquid soap, 1 tablespoon of glycerine, 5 shakes of rose essential oil and 5 shakes of geranium essential oil. Or you could use essential oil of peppermint, chamomile, lavender or petitgrain. Decant into a storage bottle. Stir or shake well before use. Stores for several months in your bathroom cabinet.

POST-SHAVE TREATMENTS

Inflammation resulting in redness, or razor burn, is a common problem. The following treatments will benefit legs as much as the face.

Garden spa

Ground elder is a potent source of vitamin C. It reduces inflammation and soothes and helps to heal cuts and abrasions. The leaves of silverweed cinquefoil can be used to make a cleansing and soothing skin lotion that eases redness. For nicks and cuts, many garden plants and weeds arrest bleeding. Try a rub of shepherd's purse or yarrow.

Post-shave skin tonic

Using a hand blender, purée an eggcup full of aloe vera sap and a crushed zinc tablet in 150ml of tonic water. Use as a tonic wash or spritz. Allow to dry naturally on skin.

Post-shave splash

Shepherd's purse soaked overnight in cider vinegar is beneficial to inflamed skin. The vinegary fragrance soon dissipates, and this can be used as a base and enhanced with a little essence of vanilla or a few shakes of your favourite essential oil.

Anti-redness/replenishing skin lotion

Blend 200ml of witch hazel extract with the scooped flesh of 1 avocado and 1 tablespoon of shea or cocoa butter. This stores well in the fridge for a week. Apply as needed to boost your skin's natural regenerative powers.

Avocado shave glaze

Avocado flesh is excellent for lessening inflammation and making your skin feel silky smooth post shave. The oil in avocado is so similar to our skin's natural oil that it has been utilised in ethnobotany as a skin-nourishing treatment for centuries. Its high content of skin-healing vitamins, including large amounts of E, A and C, make it a great treatment for razor grazes.

Shave-less glaze

Lavender and tea tree slow hair growth, while soya delays hair emergence. To 3 tablespoons of puréed aloe vera add 5 shakes of lavender essential oil, 4 shakes of tea tree essential oil and 2 tablespoons of soya (oil or milk) and stir well. Apply post shave.

PLUCKING/TWEEZING

Plucking is the method of choice for removing individual stray hairs once they are long enough to be grasped with tweezers and plucked out, removing the root and shaft. The drawback is that the follicle can become inflamed and this can result in redness in areas where a lot of hairs have been plucked, for example the eyebrows.

Top tip

A facial steam or hot-towel compress prior to plucking will open pores and make plucking easier and cause the follicle to be less harshly jolted.

Plucking is not painless and not without potential pitfalls, not least pitting or ingrown hairs (see page 99). Pluck is a bad term, as it connotes yanking out. Rather you should grip the hair as close to the root as possible with the tweezers, without pinching the skin, and gently yet firmly pull the hair out. Think of it as the difference between pulling the trigger and squeezing the trigger!

Garden spa

The juice of chickweed, cleavers, aloe and sage are all calming to plucked follicles. Just tear and squeeze the stems and foliage to get their beneficial juices.

THREADING

This is a plucking method for patches of hair rather than individual hairs. Threading is a skilled process that involves snaring or entwining unwanted hairs in taut twists of thread and pulling the hair out with the root intact. It is less painful than tweezing and somewhat less irritating to the skin/follicle. Its main benefit is the removal of fine hairs, but like any removal method it can cause redness and folliculitis (see page 98).

Anti-inflammation lotion

Calendula, chickweed, comfrey, chamomile or any other anti-inflammatory plants can be infused in a carrier oil of your choice and the oil can then be used to make an anti-inflammatory lotion (see page 38 for instructions on how to make a lotion). You can pack the jar of oil with as much herbage as fits and with more than one variety if you like. Sit the jar in a sunny window for two weeks or heat the oil and herbs in a bain-marie to speed up the extraction of plant phytochemicals.

WAXING

This involves the application of warm wax to the skin. Then the wax is covered with cloth and quickly ripped off, bringing the wax-covered hairs with it. The issue with this method is the instant pain and the inflammation afterwards. The level of pain is dependent on your pain threshold, but no matter what that might be, the waxed area will be red and sensitive for a few hours after treatment. This method is predominantly used to remove hair from the legs and the bikini line.

If you are on prescription retinoids, your skin may be too sensitive to wax. All skin types can develop sensitivity to chemical waxing, so sugaring (see page 94) might be a better option in the long-term. Folliculitis (see page 98) can be an issue.

Garden spa

Pain-easing teas can be sipped before and after treatment. Meadowsweet tea is a floral 'aspirin' and fennel seed tea contains sixteen pain-killing phytochemicals and twenty-seven antispasmodic compounds. Valerian is somewhat sedative but it also reduces sensitivity in nerve endings, while chamomile calms the skin when applied topically, and when drunk as a tea it relaxes the mind.

Kitchen spa

The capsaicin in chilli peppers depletes our body's store of substance P, a compound that conveys pain to the central nervous system. Have some for lunch or use it in an infused oil or a home-made lotion as a topical treatment. Turmeric, which is rich in curcumin, lowers the levels of the enzymes that cause inflammation.

Post-wax gels

Aloe vera gel smoothes and moisturises the skin. It is both a painkiller and an anti-inflammatory. You can make a solution to treat inflammation and pain by adding some witch hazel or capsicum oil to aloe vera gel. You could also make a paste using turmeric and aloe sap, or a cooling blend of mint leaves and aloe.

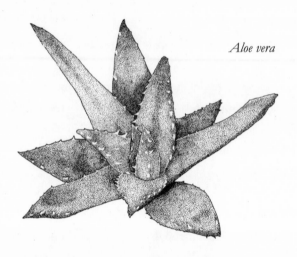

Aloe vera

SUGARING

Sugaring is an epilation method and is quite similar to waxing. It is growing in favour as the technique uses lower temperatures than waxing and it is easier to do at home, as sugar is not only hypoallergenic and antibacterial but also water-soluble. That said, inflammation is not that unusual and some care is still required with temperature. The process involves using a substrate of heated sugar, lemon juice and water on some fabric in order for it to stick to hair but not the skin and so lift (rip!) hairs out when removed. When it comes to pain, see waxing, but also note that expletives seem to dull the sensation. I find that if I 'eff' in response to striking my thumb with a hammer, the pain goes quicker than if I am in company and can't use such colourful language. Appropriate to this method, you can always shout 'Sugar!'

Sugaring paste for hair removal

Ingredients
- ¼ cup water
- ¼ cup lemon juice
- 2 cups sugar

You will also need
- cooking thermometer
- wooden spatula
- strips of cotton or muslin fabric

Method
Put the water and lemon juice in a saucepan and bring to a gentle simmer. Add the sugar and stir through until fully dissolved. Then increase the heat to bring the mixture to about 120°C. Keep stirring, avoiding hot splatters. The mixture will take on a golden colour. Remove from the heat and carefully pour into a

heatproof glass bowl. Allow the paste to cool to a point that it is still pliable but not uncomfortably hot.

Apply the paste as you would a hot wax, i.e. gather some onto the spatula and slather a thin layer onto the area of hair to be removed. Spread in the direction of the growth. Cover the pasted area with cotton/muslin strips and rub down firmly in the direction of hair growth. It will need to sit for 1 minute, so continue to the next strip. After 1 minute pull the area of skin taut with one hand, and with the other hand quickly rip off each strip, pulling backwards, in the opposite direction of hair growth. Reapply as needed (you can warm the paste in a bain-marie if the mixture becomes too cool to spread, or add some hot water if the mixture is too thick).

Note: Always exercise extreme caution when using hot-sugar solutions.

Alternative application method

When at room temperature, the mix requires kneading and stretching to make it into a soft toffee-like ball. During this process, lightly wet your hands to keep the mixture pliable and prevent it from sticking to your palms. The ball can now be stretched tightly over the area to be waxed and then swiftly removed, without the use of fabric strips. Knead again and reapply. Any surplus paste can be stored in an airtight jar in the refrigerator for several weeks. Reheat to just above room temperature and then cool to room temperature as needed.

REGROWTH DELAY

As all of these removal methods are temporary, the question of how to slow regrowth between treatments arises. The garden and kitchen can yield some help with this. Dyer's broom contains the phytoestrogen genistein, which can potentially decrease hair growth by 60–80 per cent. It is suitable for use in topically applied infusions or lotions. Genistein is also present in soya products, which can be used in lotions, masks or even in exfoliating or moisturising bases.

Hair-delay butter

There are two parts to this one. Firstly infuse 1 cup of chopped lavender (foliage and flowers) into 1 cup of soybean oil and allow to infuse for two weeks on a sunny window ledge.

Once the infused oil is ready, cold soak (i.e. overnight in a fridge) ½ cup of chamomile tops in 1 cup of soya milk. The next day, strain to remove the solids from both the milk mixture and the oil. Return the milk to the fridge to chill, and then warm 50ml of the infused oil in a bain-marie with 15g of emulsifying wax until melted together. Remove from the heat and add 50ml of the chilled soya milk. Whip with an electric whisk until thick. Allow to set in the fridge. This will keep in the fridge for two weeks. Can be utilized as a leave-on moisturiser or worn as a 30-minute treatment – rinse off with warm water and pat dry.

See also the *Shave-less glaze* on page 90 and the *Un-brow cream/ lotion* on page 103.

HAIR-REMOVAL PROBLEMS

You can find treatments for redness in the section on shaving (page 87), but redness is an inflammatory response to agitation of the skin or follicle and can be a result of any method of hair removal. Below are some other conditions that can arise (often in conjunction with redness) no matter what technique of hair removal you use.

FOLLICULITIS

Folliculitis is an inflamed follicle or follicles, often triggered by infection caused by bacteria, fungus or even insect bites, resulting in raised red bumps (somewhat acne-like in appearance), which are sometimes pus-filled and which sometimes develop into itchy rash-like patches. Shaving can worsen folliculitis. Men tend to develop it on the face while women most often experience it on their legs. That said, on average your body has around five million hair follicles distributed across your skin's surface and folliculitis can occur on any one of them. Some body moisturisers and make-up can block and irritate follicles, causing a folliculitis flare-up.

Thyme

Garden spa

It is often too difficult to distinguish between bacterial and fungal infections, but many natural garden antibiotics are also antimicrobials and will deal with either. Try a thyme tincture or a thyme rinse.

INGROWN HAIR

An ingrown hair is invisible to the naked eye but as it develops it manifests as a small bump, often itchy and red and occasionally pus-filled. Sometimes you might notice a curled or contorted hair emerging from the centre of the bump. The process of shaving is often responsible for ingrown hairs, as they occur because a sliced-off hair shaft grows back into the follicle rather than out of it.

Hot-towel treatments or facial steams pre- or post-shave can prevent ingrown hairs by opening up the pores so that the freshly cut shaft can point outwards, in the right direction.

HERBAL PORE OPENERS

Pores don't open and close like valves. They seem larger when clogged up and smaller when free of debris. In keeping with beauty-spa terminology we can say a facial steam 'opens' pores via its debris-loosening, skin-cleansing, pore-degunking action, but a steam facial of fennel or eucalyptus can 'open' pores and assist further by being antibacterial. See also *Facial steam* on page 33.

RAZOR BURN

Razor burn is a rash caused by the scrape of the blade. Shaving with the grain minimises this, as does a good shaving balm or gel that helps the blade to glide. Rinse the blade between every pass and rinse your face after shaving with a room-temperature anti-inflammatory green and mint tea or meadowsweet hydrosol.

RAZOR BUMPS AND BARBER'S ITCH

Razor bumps are sometimes a side effect of shaving. The localised inflamed bumps are the result of ingrown hairs. See *Ingrown hair* on page 99.

Barber's itch (*pseudofolliculitis barbae*) is a post-shave itch related not to razor burn but to the bacteria *Staphylococcus*.

Garden spa

Essential oil of tea tree used topically is great, but other herbal treatments for *Staphylococcus* include tinctures of goldenseal, burdock root, dandelion root or echinacea. Use these externally as a rub or compress, or, using a dropper, you can add 2–5ml to a glass of water 3–4 times daily for a week. A tincture of burdock seeds is particularly strong and effective. Crush the seeds first. Hyssop tea is an antiviral and will boost the immune system when taken internally, but if mixed with chamomile and cleaver juice it can soothe and deep cleanse the areas affected by barber's itch topically.

Kitchen spa

Diluted apple cider vinegar can be used as a facial splash. A mask of manuka honey is also helpful.

TRICKY HAIRS/PROBLEM AREAS

Individual rogue hairs happen to both sexes and in the most random places sometimes. A scissor trim or using tweezers often rectifies the problem. If using tweezers, take care not to damage the follicle with jerky extraction – aim for one swift movement.

FEMALE FACIAL HAIR

Do not shave it! Shaving always results in harsh stubble regrowth. Laser, electrolysis, threading, waxing and depilatory creams/agents formulated for use on facial hair are better options. Some women opt to bleach rather than remove hair but I would worry about the chemicals in that method. See the kitchen spa for upper-lip hair overleaf for a natural alternative.

Essential-oil treatments

Both lavender and tea tree essential oils may have anti-androgenic properties and are a brilliantly simple solution to treating excessive hair growth on androgen-dependent areas of a woman's body (face, chin and breasts particularly). Any salve, lotion or cream recipe in this book can be made anti-androgenic by adding 1 tablespoon each of lavender and tea tree oils. Silcock's Base or other emollient creams, or even petroleum jelly (if ethics and allergy status allow), can be medicated with these oils and used as night treatments. Those oils are also safe to add to any of the masks or skin peels in this book.

UPPER-LIP HAIR (WOMEN)

Traditional hair-removal methods are temporary and some actually thicken hairs. Laser and electrolysis tend to work best with darker hair.

Garden spa

While the garden gives us aloe and other plant gels to minimise post-treatment redness, and also lavender to infuse in oil for its anti-androgenic and hair-softening effect, the kitchen can best stretch the time between appointments and maybe even tackle the issues directly.

Kitchen spa

A mask with a soya-milk or soybean base may have some potential to lighten upper-lip hair in more ways than one. Soya contains protease inhibitors and therefore reduces tyrosinase and TRP-1 protein levels, thus slowing the growth of hair and reducing the thickness of the shaft. It also reduces pigmentation in the hair follicle, making hair appear finer, shorter and more transparent.

UNIBROWS

Plucking with tweezers, professional threading, home waxing or sugaring will all put a divide between your brows, but once you start any of these, the fear is that removal can thicken hairs and make the brow more pronounced. The isoflavones in soya exert an oestrogenic effect that curtails growth, so applying soya directly or as part of a home-made treatment (lotions, creams, masks, etc.) between removal treatments will slow the growth and thin regrowing hairs.

Un-brow cream/lotion (with anti-androgenic and hair shaft-shrinking effects)

There are two steps to this. First infuse some hair-shrinking phytochemicals from lavender, chamomile or fenugreek seeds in hormone-stabilising soybean oil for two to three weeks on a sunny window ledge (or heat for 20 minutes in a lidded jam jar sat in water that has been brought to the boil and then removed from the heat. Repeat this each day for three days).

Step two is to make the cream/lotion. In a bain-marie melt together ½ cup of infused oil and ½ cup of emulsifying wax grains. Remove from the heat, pour in ½ cup of cold soya milk and stir well. Refrigerate for 10 minutes. Remove from the fridge and stir well. Refrigerate for a further 10 minutes and then stir well again. Repeat these two steps until the mixture reaches your desired consistency. If you prefer, you can whip with an electric whisk after the second cooling spell. This sets harder if stored in the fridge, where it will keep for two weeks.

FACIAL SKINCARE AND CONDITIONS

With the exception of the chest area, the skin on your face is thinner than the skin anywhere else on your body. The facial epidermis is around 0.12mm thick, while body skin is closer to 0.60mm. Also, body skin has fewer sebaceous glands, so oiliness and other conditions that affect the face are less of an issue in body care. As such the formulations here are designed for the face but can also be used on other areas of the body. See the section on body skin for advice on maintaining the rest of your skin and on body-specific conditions.

The thinness of the fat layer of the face makes it easier for wrinkles to form there. The fact that the face is generally exposed makes it susceptible to sun damage and other environmental stresses. Facial skin is particularly rich in pores, which has two significant implications: evaporation (moisture and electrolytes are lost quicker from the face than elsewhere on your body) and toxic secretion (sweat removes internal impurities to the surface of skin). So while pimples and surface blemishes can occur anywhere, they are more likely to affect the face. Cleansing, toning and moisturising are key to facial health and radiance, and I will explore options specific to different skin types over the following pages.

While there is a difference between male and female skin

(women have considerably fewer active hair follicles and their skin tends to be smoother in texture), the remedies here are geared to skin type or condition rather than being gender specific. Duration of application could be lengthened for men with particularly tough skin. Whether you're male or female, the best thing you can do for your face is apply sunscreen when venturing outside in daylight. It doesn't just prevent sunburn, but also premature ageing!

NORMAL SKIN

Some may argue that normal skin is not so much a skin type but a kind of equilibrium that we may achieve at different times in our life – an ideal, balanced, finely textured surface with a healthy glow and no open pores. It is what those with dry or oily skin aim for and what cosmetic products and beauty treatments promise. I would argue that most of us have combination skin, a mix of different types in different places, but if you are one of those lucky enough to have sustained 'normal' skin, it is as much to do with your pH as it is with other factors such as skincare regime, age, hydration, general health, etc.

Normal skin sits between 5.6 and 6 on the pH scale, which as gardeners we know is slightly acidic, thanks mainly to the presence of gentle acids in the face's sebum, sweat and keratin. Maintaining the optimal acidity level of the skin can be as simple as swapping to a vinegar toner or a cleanser with a lemon juice base.

Normal skin sounds ideal but it has its own issues. It can

age quicker than oilier skin due to less sebaceous activity, which means it is not kept naturally moisturised. When you think about it, greasy skin is oily by nature and we correct dry skin by adding oil, but normal skin is not recognised as a squeaky wheel. You need to take precautions to avoid premature ageing under eyes in particular, an area with almost zero sebaceous activity (see *Wrinkles* on page 153).

Garden spa

Calendula, chamomile, lavender, rose, elderflower, linden blossom, peony and even garden daisy all complement normal skin and, when made into hydrosols, they are great antidotes to hard water or harsh products. Use them in rinses or spritzes, as hydrosols or as simple tea-infusions. The floral waters can also be made into lotions to extend your care regime.

Chamomile

Kitchen spa

Invest in an ionizer/filter or let a jug of tap water sit overnight to self-filter. Drink several glasses of water a day to top up internal hydration, and make a skin-refreshing green tea spritz with the rest, to keep skin hydrated throughout the day. Both honey masks and oatmeal masks feed and moisturise the skin, while fruit masks have rejuvenating properties. Remember to watch what you eat, avoiding junk foods and processed foods loaded with bad fats, preservatives, salt and sugar.

Rose water and yeast cleansing mask for normal skin

Make a paste using 3 teaspoons of rose water and 2 teaspoons of brewer's yeast. Add more or less of either ingredient to achieve the consistency you prefer. Apply in gentle circular motions and leave on for 10–15 minutes. Rinse off with tepid water and pat dry with a kitchen towel.

Petal-perfect toner

Submerge elderflowers and chamomile in witch hazel extract and soak for one week. Shake regularly. After a week, strain to remove the solids. Use as you would a standard toner. All three ingredients promote even skin tone and help to maintain normal skin and regulate sebum balance.

Buttermilk, almond and avocado blitz

A moisturising, clarifying cleanser
Simply blitz ½ cup of buttermilk with the scooped out flesh of ½ an avocado and 2 tablespoons of ground almonds or chickpea flour. Chill and apply with your fingers, using a circular motion. Leave for 10–15 minutes and remove with a damp cloth or herbal rinse of your choice.

DRY SKIN

Toil in soil (sandy or not) and exposure to drying winds mean dry skin is common in gardeners. UV damage (see page 148) also exacerbates dryness. Extreme weather and even just the seasonal dips and highs can affect production of sebum (the skin's natural barrier) and allow moisture to evaporate. Dry skin may manifest as chapped lips (see page 179), chapped hands (see page 247) or even rough elbows (see page 241), all of which are dealt with in these pages.

Dry facial skin is characterised by tautness caused by a lack of moisture in the upper layers of the skin and a paucity of sebum in the lower layers. The visible flaking of skin can begin around the nose and with patches of eyebrow dandruff (or for men with itchy scaling in the moustache or beard), soon developing into a roughness or scaling on the cheeks and even the forehead and at the hairline. Ignoring dry skin can lead to premature ageing of the skin and the early emergence of fine lines (see *Wrinkles* on page 153).

Top tip

UV rays can penetrate quicker and deeper into dry and dehydrated skin than other skin types, increasing the risk of sun damage and drying skin even further, so always use a good sunblock that both protects and moisturises. Look out for products that contain plenty of aloe vera or cocoa butter.

Garden spa

Many flowers and garden herbs have a long history of use in treating dry skin, including daisies, marshmallow, borage, lady's mantle, calendula and rose. Succulent plants such as aloe vera, sedum and *Sempervivums* have also been used in natural moisturisers for centuries.

Kitchen spa

It is all too easy to lose skin oils if your diet is too low in fat. Making a salad dressing oil with calendula petals (packed with luteins and vitamin A) turns a tasty lunch into a therapeutic meal. Eating avocados, butternut squash, carrots, sweet potatoes and other foods packed with antioxidant carotenoids will also bolster skin health. Most of these make great facials too. Just pulp or blitz them in a blender with a drop of green tea for consistency and an extra antioxidant boost.

Calendula moisturising cream

The glycosides and saponins in calendula are very effective cleansing and antiseptic agents but they also help reduce inflammation, soothe irritated tissue, hydrate and promote skin-healing. All the other ingredients hydrate too. In a mortar and pestle crush 2 tablespoons of calendula petals with ½ teaspoon of water and 2 tablespoons of fresh dairy cream. You can also use the calendula oil to make a lotion/cream.

Rose and cucumber toning mask

Rose petals are cleansing, stimulating and soothing. Their astringent quality means that they tone and their natural hydrating effect upon skin makes them an ideal ingredient to treat dry skin, as well as ageing skin, psoriasis and eczema, etc. Cucumbers are a great source of pantothenic acid (vitamin B5), which, along with the active ingredients of cucurbitacin and cucumerin contained in its juice and flesh, helps hydrate skin. Yoghurt is beneficial to balance the skin's pH.

Ingredients

- 80g cucumber
- petals of 1 rose head
- 80g natural yoghurt
- almond flour (optional)

Method

Wash the cucumber (peel if store-bought and you suspect residual chemicals) and then slice or chop it. Put it in a blender with the rose petals and yoghurt and blend to a pulp. You can thicken the mixture with almond flour if you like. Apply to your face fresh from the blender and leave on for up to 15 minutes (at least 5 minutes). Rinse off and pat the skin dry. The surplus mixture will store in the fridge for up to three days.

GREASY/OILY SKIN AND SEBORRHOEA

A greasy skin type typically presents with open pores and an oily surface, which predisposes one to pimples (see page 128), blackheads (see page 128) and potentially also acne (see page 130). But before you despair, there is some good news: 'oiliness' of itself will keep your skin looking younger for longer. The first trick is to prevent dirt and bacteria from causing blackheads and more worrisome pore-damaging issues. The second trick is to not rely too much on commercial products, which chemically strip the top layers of skin in the process of treating oiliness, or indeed on harsh home-made remedies not recommended in this book. Both will result in the loss of too much moisture and your sebum glands will only produce more oil to counteract that.

Greasy skin is simply the result of the overproduction of sebum, the oily substance secreted by the natural oil glands in the lower layers of the skin. The normal role of sebum is to lubricate the skin against friction and to act as a waterproof barrier – to prevent the loss of water from your body. It also protects your skin from bacterial and fungal infections.

You may naturally have oily skin or it may be a result of your lifestyle. For instance, too much secretion can be caused by a harsh beauty regime or by using inappropriate skincare products for your skin type or by being overenthusiastic with their application. Some cosmetics and oil-based make-ups can clog pores or generate oiliness themselves. Fast food and a fat-laden diet are not helpful. It's not just the bad fats but also the iodine and other chemicals that can contribute to spots and other reactions. Also, if your gastrointestinal tract is overloaded it has no other recourse but to send excess fat to the sebum glands for elimination.

Garden spa

Many common culinary herbs such as rosemary, thyme, mint and yarrow are natural astringents and make excellent face washes or spritzes to close pores and regulate sebum release. All four also help to combat bacteria, cleanse and clarify. Calendula flowers are often used in skin preparations where cell regeneration is called for, but also in infusion washes or petal poultices that regularise and normalise the production of sebaceous secretions. Employing calendula oil does all that and deep cleanses.

A paste of jasmine flowers (or essential oil of jasmine if you don't grow this fragrant gem) increases blood circulation to the skin, not only bringing oxygen and nutrients into the cells but detoxifying them too. This is brilliant in creams or masks to help control overactive oil glands. Rock rose is a strong astringent and is cleansing too. Used in a vinegar or hydrosol, it would be beneficial to greasy skin. Aloe has the potential to moisturise dry skin, but it can also be used to clean and moisturise greasy skin without leaving it feeling oily.

Kitchen spa

Olive oil as a face cleanser may sound like a far-fetched, frugal attempt at a home-made beauty product, but not only is olive oil remedial to skin, it is the perfect choice for greasy skin and, far from being parsimonious, its inclusion in your routine is prudent. You have heard the saying *fight fire with fire*; well, in a sense this is what it does. The truth is that simple washing does not work with greasy skin as oil and water don't mix; this is why many commercial facial washes have chemicals and solvents to degrease your face. But oil and oil do mix. The olive oil, while feeding your skin's vitality, mixes with the sebum, dirt and all that gunk we call grease, so that when you wipe it away with a cotton pad or cloth it takes the bad stuff with it.

Enthused oil-infused cleanser

Why should only teeth and feet get the peppermint tingle? Torn and infused in some olive oil (for one to two weeks), peppermint generates a fresh feeling but is also an antibacterial cleanser for greasy skin. Combine with the extra punch of healing and sebum-controlling calendula for a super treatment.

Method
Simply add 4 calendula petals to ½ cup of torn/chopped peppermint in a jam jar or Kilner jar, cover completely with olive oil and allow to infuse on a sunny window ledge for at least one week. You can continue the infusing process until the calendula petals lose their colour, yielding a more potent oil. Then strain to remove the solids. Store in the bathroom cabinet and use as part of your daily regime or as a regular night-time cleanse.

Jasmine, rose and witch hazel floral facial toner

This is a natural solution for oily skin, helping to detox skin cells and regulate sebum production. It is also a tonic for ageing skin, sensitive skin, combination skin and acne.

Ingredients

- 2 tablespoons fresh jasmine flowers
- 2 tablespoons vegetable glycerine
- ⅓ cup rose water (see page 143)
- ⅓ cup witch hazel extract (see page 55)

Method

Use a blender to combine the ingredients. Apply as you would a normal toner. This also makes a great base for salt masks (see *Acne* on page 130). Any surplus will store in the fridge for 3 days, and longer if you substitute essential oil for the fresh jasmine flowers. Shake well before use.

COMBINATION SKIN

Combination skin is simply a mix of the oily and dry patches we all experience at some time in our life. For those whose skin is nearly always combination, it tends to be the T-zone (the forehead, nose and often the chin) that has a propensity towards a lot of sebum production – thus becoming oily – while the rest of the face seems to lack moisture and consequentially suffers not just a taut dryness but flakiness too.

Top tip

Not all combination-skin types conform to the T-zone division, but wherever the combination occurs don't waste your time or money on different cleansers, toners and moisturisers for different areas. Instead opt for a general water-and-glycerine-based product. Your T-zone should benefit from cleansing twice a day but the dry patches will only need to be cleansed once a day. The opposite is true when it comes to moisturising.

Regular but not obsessive exfoliation is a great treatment for combination skin. Most beauty clinics and salons use a beta-hydroxy acid (BHA) treatment as it not only exfoliates and replenishes the surface skin but also exfoliates and cleanses inside each pore while helping to rectify any damage from over- or under-production of sebum. As gardeners we have many plants growing that can deliver a BHA treatment, and the fridge, fruit bowl and pantry can offer solutions too.

Garden spa

Make your own BHA treatment using homegrown fruits or garden plants and herbs that contain salicylic acid (e.g. meadowsweet, willow, etc.). Rose petals are remedial to both oily and dry skin, so they're perfect for combination skin. You could make a petal compress or a petal lotion. You could blitz some petals in a little yoghurt or honey as a mask, or distil some rose water to keep as a spritz. Chamomile tea is also great to cleanse combination skin.

Treatments for dry skin (see page 108) can treat your dry zones while oily zones can be remedied by the garden herbs and plants listed for greasy skin (see page 111).

Kitchen spa

Most soft fleshy fruits make excellent face masks and deliver BHA, but papaya is particularly good at preventing both the enlarged pores and the blackheads that are common with combination skin. Strawberry is not only exfoliating but also replenishing, and it promotes cellular regeneration. These same fruits contain alpha-hydroxy acids (AHA), which are a natural exfoliant but also have anti-inflammatory properties to soothe skin after exfoliation. AHAs are present in dairy products, so cream can follow or accompany a strawberry mask.

Lemon steam ahead

Put ½ a cup of foliage of lemon balm and the juice of ½ a lemon in a basin. Pour over boiling water. Make a towel tent over your head to keep the steam from dissipating, and allow the herbal steam to open your pores and revitalise the sebaceous glands. Do not use steam if you have thread veins; make as a face wash instead.

Honey milk face glaze

Mix 2 tablespoons of honey with 1 tablespoon of full-fat milk (full-fat has more lactic acid and amino acids). Apply to the face and leave for 15 minutes before rinsing with tepid water.

Peony and parsley face paste

The protein, vitamin C, sulphur, and chlorophyll found in parsley can really cleanse your skin, and peony petals encourage regeneration and a healthy glow. Blitz equal quantities of herb and flower and use as a 10–20-minute mask.

Parsley

Note: Parsley is used to lighten freckles. It can have a whitening effect on some skins.

SENSITIVE SKIN

Sensitive skin can be hereditary or it can develop at any stage in your life. Sometimes the sensitivity can come and go. Permanent or temporary, the symptoms are the same. But there is a silver lining – the treatments are effective for both.

Sensitive skin can be prone to redness and reaction, sometimes due to allergens or the harshness of products, but often just due to the environmental stresses of drying wind, hot sun, cold, or even office air conditioning or home central heating. It can be more prone to the effects of these stressors as it can often be rather thin/fine in texture, leading more quickly to pore, skin-cell and capillary damage. Redness and broken veins are symptomatic. You may also be more prone to sunburn (see page 149). Always opt for fragrance-free, hypoallergenic products; the fewer ingredients the better. Hydration and moisturisation are key, as well-fed and hydrated skin generates its own barriers to environmental stress. So keep hydrated from within and moisturised on the outside.

Garden spa

Lavender, calendula and chamomile are soothing to skin. Use them in rinses or as remedy ingredients in salves, lotions or creams. Borage is moisturising, and the old reliable, roses, yield a soothing moisturiser too, when blended with some cucumber slices or a little aloe vera sap to make a pamper mask. You could try a quick fix of vegetable glycerine and rose water (see page 143) as a soothing night gel.

Top tip

Antihistamine teas are beneficial where sensitive skin occurs seasonally or is a reaction. Try lemon balm, thyme, fennel or echinacea, as well as green tea, chamomile tea, ginger or nettle tea. A chilled or iced tea of any of these, or a combo of two or more, is delicious.

Kitchen spa

Cleanse with whole milk, as dairy fats also replenish skin. Oatmeal face masks are great for sensitive skin. Try a smoothie with any of the herbal teas above as a base and plumped up with apples and strawberries, both rich in natural antihistamines and packed with the potent antioxidant flavonoid quercetin, itself a strong antihistamine.

Note: Quite a lot of common emollients and humectants in commercial products have been linked to flare-ups or can cause allergic reactions in people with sensitive skin. Not all of these emollients and humectants come from plant sources. That said, some people are very sensitive and can be sensitive to natural products too, so do a patch test first.

Chamomile and green tea face wash

Chamomile is cleansing and restorative, while green tea helps to loosen dead skin cells and remove them to reveal new skin underneath. Simply make a cup of green tea as normal but add a handful of chamomile petals to the infusion while still hot. Once cooled, use as a facial rinse. This can be refrigerated for one week and makes an excellent facial spritz to refresh when your nose is to the grindstone or your eyeballs are glued to the computer screen. Hard work and electromagnetic fields can have an impact on skin health. You don't have to be lazy or stone age, just treat yourself from time to time.

Roman chamomile toner is strongly anti-inflammatory and is soothing too, so it's especially suitable for sensitive skin. Make as a tea-wash or a hydrosol.

Coconut oil moisturiser can cause less of a sensitive response than other vegetable oils. Use it unadulterated or alternatively infuse it with the skin-soothing

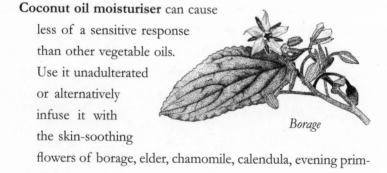

Borage

flowers of borage, elder, chamomile, calendula, evening primrose or rose.

COMPLEXION

Complexion is a term that has come to signify health and beauty. Pale or pallid skin gives you away as sick or sun shy; rosy cheeks indicate health, youth or the flights of stairs you just ran up. In the beauty industry, complexion is everything. It is what creates the demand for toners, clarifiers, tinted moisturisers, etc.

In essence, complexion is whatever is the natural (long-term or in the moment) colour tone, texture, and overall appearance of your skin. It is interesting to note that the word *complexion* originally referred to the medieval concept that our constitution is made up of a combination of the four humours – cold, heat, moistness and dryness – all factors that affect skin, especially the face.

Better complexion is achieved through a healthy lifestyle. Get some exercise, some fresh air in your lungs, stay hydrated and eat good quality, nutritious food. Also adopt a good skincare regime – cleanse, tone and moisturise.

Garden spa

A decoction of dandelion flowers makes a great lotion for body and face, while a spring salad of dandelion leaves is said to rejuvenate one's complexion too (note that the leaves can be too bitter to eat later in the year). An array of complexion washes can be made with a decoction of lady's mantle flowers, linden flowers, cowslips, elderflowers or clary sage. The ancient Egyptians soaked lupin seeds in water,

Cowslips

and during Roman times mullein soaked in milk was popular as a cleanser.

Kitchen spa

Some foods are good for your complexion. Flaxseed, apart from being packed with healthy omega 3 fatty acids that fight spots and blemishes, also improves the natural irrigation of skin cells, boosting hydration and helping to detoxify – the two keys to an even, radiant complexion. Walnuts are good too, if you prefer.

Top tip

I do mention green tea a lot in this book; it's the beneficial catechins that are so potently antioxidant, anti-inflammatory and that switch on our natural defences to weight gain, cellular degeneration and even cancer. Two or more cups a day can even out complexion and skin texture too. I am a fan of the flavour of iced green tea in summer and hot green tea in winter. But if you have a wedding or job interview on the horizon and you want to look your best, here's a trick nobody tells you – hot is better, as those antioxidants start to degrade as the tea cools. Hot, not scalding. Let it steep for 7 minutes to completely extract the healing compounds. Don't ignore the benefits of the iced version or the cooled version in shampoos and facial rinses, but to kick start a complexion rescue, have it hot with a slice of lemon (lemon also helps its absorption into the bloodstream).

SALLOW SKIN

Sallow skin is generally described as dull and unhealthy-looking, referring to both its colour/tone and texture. Weekly exfoliation can go a long way to brightening a dull complexion. Sallow skin can indicate underlying issues (kidney problems, ulcers, etc.) or highlight a simple iron deficiency. If you also have symptoms such as dizziness, tiredness, insomnia, a pale tongue or an erratic pulse, make an appointment with your GP to get to the root of it.

Garden spa

The simple solution to sallow skin is to eat your five a day. The moisture and phytochemicals in fruit and veg have a direct correlation with the skin's appearance. A mask of aloe vera and mint is replenishing. Mix 1 tablespoon of calendula oil with 1 tablespoon of puréed cooked tomato and 1 teaspoon of poppy or nigella seeds to make a great face scrub that refreshes the skin. A spritz of the tisane or hydrosol of daisy, dandelion or elderflower all help to enliven a sallow complexion.

Kitchen spa

Sallow skin can be the result of poor nutrition and inadequate hydration. Healthy smoothies and meals that incorporate fruit and vegetables can supply both moisture and nutrients to the skin from within. Many can also be used as face masks, doing good on the surface and in the layers beneath. A brewer's yeast face mask (mixed with a little water or egg white) is a good skin treatment and can rectify some B vitamin deficiencies if you sprinkle it on your cereal.

PORES: VISIBLE AND BLOCKED

You may just have about five million of these 'openings' in the skin. Pores are really the entrance to hair follicles, and the terms *follicle* and *pore* are pretty interchangeable. Not every pore has a visible hair shaft and we often tend to think of them as how our skin breathes. These tiny blowholes in reality are the moisturising/waterproofing mechanism of your body, allowing sebum to come to the surface of the skin.

It's when they get bunged up with dirt, bacteria or dead cells that problems arise – pimples, boils and the dreaded large pores. Any astringent herbs in a wash or steam (see opposite) will shrink them back after you have cleansed with a facial cleanser suited to your skin type. Regular exfoliation is key.

It never rains but it pores tonic

The three great pore refiners are yarrow, viola and witch hazel. Simply immerse the aerial parts of yarrow and viola (in equal parts) in a bottle/jar of witch hazel extract until it is full. Leave overnight before first use. Allow it to continue infusing/maturing for several months and use as you go.

Coconut and brown sugar scrub

Simply mix 1 tablespoon each of coconut oil and brown sugar in the palm of your hand and apply to your skin with your fingers using circular motions. This exfoliates and moisturises at the same time. Rinse your face when finished and pat dry.

Herbs for facial steams

Add crushed or chopped herb (or essential oil) to a basin of boiling water. Make a tent with a towel over your head so that the steam is trapped and you get the full benefit. Not advised if you have thread veins.

Blackberry leaves promote sebum control and replenish oily skin

Chamomile is cleansing and soothing

Cranesbill is astringent and soothing

Comfrey root and leaf are healing

Cowslip petals are a tonic

Bistort is an astringent

Dandelion root is stimulating and restorative; also a tonic

Elderflower is toning and stimulating

Fennel removes impurities

Geranium is soothing and balancing

Green tea is rejuvenating and refreshing

Lavender is soothing and has antibiotic properties

Linden flowers remove impurities and act as a tonic

Mint is stimulating and toning

Nettle removes impurities and boosts circulation

Bistort

Raspberry leaves assist sebum control and replenish oily skin

Rosemary is cleansing and boosts circulation

Sage is stimulating and toning

Strawberry foliage promotes sebum control and replenishes oily skin

Thyme is antibacterial and cleansing

Yarrow is astringent

Both rose water and witch hazel are great for 'closing' pores after a steam treatment.

PUFFY FACE

A late night, or a restless one, can bloat the face as much as a reaction to environmental stresses. Even the pressure of the pillow against your skin can do it. A cold compress (a damp facecloth chilled in the fridge, or slices of chilled cucumber laid directly on the skin) will help reduce some puffiness while your body tackles it in its own fashion. If that fashion is too slow for your liking, the solutions below should speed up the process. Very often a puffy face is a hydration issue and that morning OJ or cuppa will begin the recovery process.

Top tip

Keep your moisturiser, toner and cleanser in the fridge. The chill takes down the swelling as much as the action of the products.

Garden spa

The garden has the whole gamut of antihistamine, anti-inflammatory plants that can be brewed into a tea and sipped to hydrate and deflate or used in spritzes or face washes. Echinacea tea or tincture are natural antihistamines but they also stimulate the lymphatic system to drain, thus eliminating toxins. Heartsease acts the same way. Tisanes of agrimony, borage, elderflower, ginkgo, mint and nettle all address puffiness when used internally or externally.

Kitchen spa

Drink water throughout the day. Water can balance any excess sodium intake and so reduce swelling. Chilled slices of veg can reduce puffiness. Plump soft fruits can hydrate and also balance nutritional deficits that trigger puffiness – wear some, munch some.

Mint

Cucumber and coffee facial

Simply make an espresso-sized cup of strong coffee and blitz it with a whole cucumber (if not homegrown, remove the skin). Wear for 20 minutes and then rinse with tepid water. Repeat daily. This keeps in the fridge for four days.

BREAK-OUTS

SPOTS AND PIMPLES, BLACKHEADS AND WHITEHEADS

There may be something about dust and soil and the blood, sweat and tears that go into making a garden perfect that can clog pores and make the gardener more susceptible to the odd breakout. But many infusions of garden plants can make cleansing rinses and act as helpful topical antibiotics to reduce bacteria in the skin – the prime cause of blackheads, whiteheads, pimples and spots.

Top tip

Essential fatty acids inhibit bacteria growth and work against both infection and inflammation. Applying them topically can allow our immune system to defend us more effectively. One of the best garden-sourced essential fatty acids is gamma-linolenic acid, which is found in evening primrose oil, borage seed oil and blackcurrant seed oil. You can make your own if you have a press, or you can use a mortar and pestle on some seeds in a little glycerine or yoghurt/kefir to release the oils. Use the crushed seed and the oil as a face scrub or mask.

Garden aid

Cleaver juice is great for all types of skin eruptions. Witch hazel extract and apple cider vinegar both make excellent pore closers and natural cleansers. You can add to either the astringent and healing benefits of dog-rose, loosestrife, sage, salvia, bearberry, blackthorn, hawthorn, oak, horse chestnut and cypress, or the antiseptic benefits of thyme, rosemary or lavender. Holy basil (and unholy varieties too) has antifungal and antibacterial properties. Infusions or pastes of plantain, mint, fennel and fennel seeds, marshmallow flower and root, yarrow tops and birch leaves are also beneficial to pore and skin function. Agrimony is a disinfectant and an astringent. A paste of mullein flowers is antiseptic.

Let's call the whole thing off tomato juice mask

For pimples and blackheads
Tomatoes pulped and used as face masks are good for any skin type but they are of huge benefit to oily, blemished or acne-affected skin. The trick here is in the juice as a delivery mechanism for the phytonutrients, mineral content and astringent. The lycopene content protects against oxidative damage, the vitamin A component will rejuvenate and the vitamin C content clarifies skin. Witch hazel boosts the astringency and Epsom salts help to flush out toxins.

Ingredients
- 50ml tomato juice
- 1 tablespoon witch hazel extract
- 1 teaspoon Epsom salts
- 1 tablespoon agar agar or other vegetable gelatine

Method

Heat the tomato juice in a bain-marie and then add all the other ingredients. Continue heating and stir until the gelatine fully dissolves. Remove from the heat and cool to room temperature. Pat onto your face (avoiding your eyes) and allow to dry completely (it may begin to naturally peel at this point). Then wash/peel off the mask.

Quick-fix zit zapper

Put 1 teaspoon of zinc ointment in an eggcup or a container of a similar size. Add 10 drops each of tea tree and lavender essential oils and stir well. After washing the site of the spot with soapy water, use as a zit shrinker and antiseptic ointment. This stores well for several months.

ACNE

Acne is a shortening of the medical name *acne vulgaris*. It's an inflammatory disorder of the sebaceous glands and hair follicles that causes excess sebum production and clogging of pores. Bacteria are at the root of the problem. Primarily affecting the face, upper back and chest, acne presents as an eruption of pimples and pustules, including blackheads. Common during adolescence and synonymous with hormonal changes, acne can persist into the late twenties. The difference between acne and a pimple breakout is the potential for cystic blemish lesions, where the pimple becomes more of a cyst or lesion and can leave behind a blemish or a pockmark scar.

Garden spa

Many herbalists employ echinacea to boost immunity or select hormone balancers such as *agnus-castus* (female) or saw palmetto (male). Hydrosols of lemon balm and bergamot make great toners for acne-affected skin. An infusion of heartsease, chamomile, calendula, goldenrod, field scabious, rose or pot geranium makes a beneficial topical skin tonic and can be used in lotions or in gentle washes. See also *Facial steam* on page 33.

Echinacea

Kitchen spa

Lemon juice diluted with rose water makes a fine facial cleanser, tackling bacteria and oiliness. The lactic acid found in milk products cleanses the skin of dirt and bacteria and balances the pH of skin so that it regenerates better. It also inhibits bacterial growth. So washing your face with milk or using a fresh-cream face mask is ideal; just be sure to hide from the cat. I would, however, recommend reducing your consumption of dairy products during flare-ups, as the hormones contained in milk can act like human androgens and so contribute to increased oil secretion.

TO WAR WITH ACNE

Using natural beauty treatments such as washes, lotions and face masks, etc. may cause an instant decrease in oiliness and create the feeling of a deep cleanse, but that's only half the battle. It may take four to six weeks to notice more serious improvements in your condition. The treatments listed here will bring the war to a close quicker.

Warpaint face mask

To combat inflammation and oxidative stress

Simply stir up ⅓ cup of tomato juice with 2 tablespoons of wheatgerm and 1 teaspoon of green tea. Apply to the face or individual spots and leave on for 10 minutes to dry. Rinse with tepid water.

Bath bombs

In a way this is like making sandcastles at the beach with slightly wet sand, but instead of a bucket and spade you use a spoon and kitchen moulds. These are great for acne on all parts of the body.

Dry ingredients

- 240g baking soda
- 120g corn starch
- 120g citric acid

- 60g Epsom salts
- 60g table/sea salt

Wet ingredients

- 1 tablespoon water (alternatively use rose water or herbal tea)
- 1 tablespoon olive oil or infused oil of your choice
- 5 shakes of your favourite essential oil (optional)

Method

Place all the dry ingredients in a glass bowl and stir well until fully combined and no clumps of a single ingredient remain. Add the oil slowly while folding through. Then add the water even more slowly – use a dropper if you have one. Keep stirring to stop the mixture beginning to fizz prematurely. Add essential oil for scent, again stirring continuously. The mixture should now be moist enough to pack into moulds (or hand shape if you have the skill). You can let it set in the mould or knock it out carefully after a few seconds. Store in an airtight container. Use within four months.

Peppermint and wild mustard bath bomb

Wild mustard accumulates selenium from the soil. Selenium protects plants from fungal infection but is great for humans too, as it is an antioxidant and an anti-inflammatory. Selenium can improve the elasticity of the skin and so reduce acne scars. Peppermint is an antifungal and it stimulates pores to detox.

Simply add 1 tablespoon of each herb, finely chopped, to the bath bomb recipe above or use peppermint essential oil and mustard-infused oil.

ACNE SCARS

There are several ways acne can scar.

TYPE 1: Sometimes even after the pimple/lesion/cyst has been successfully treated – the bacteria eliminated, the sebum under control and the pus or head of the pimple eradicated – there can remain a slight red dot. This is part of the healing process and generally fades beyond visibility within six to twelve months. Sometimes this hyperpigmentation does not fade, in which case your GP may refer you to a dermatologist, often for ALA (alpha-lipoic acid), AHA or BHA treatments (all chemicals extracted from plants) or microdermabrasion.

TYPE 2: Other times the pimple/lesion/cyst leaves behind a scar – generally a dimple or puncture hole in the skin where the collagen has been damaged in the cell wall of the once-infected pore. This damage can potentially be lessened with vitamin A and E night masks, but the jury is out on the effectiveness of these on acne scars. Certainly there is no harm in a dietary intake of antioxidants (including vitamins A and E), combined with many of the nourishing masks and rejuvenating lotions contained in this book that employ AHAs and BHAs. Popping pustules, squeezing pimples, picking scabs and scratching blackheads can all contribute to scarring.

TYPE 3: Unfortunately some acne scars are of the rolling, or undulating, variety and have caused damage to the subcutaneous tissue below the surface skin. Home treatments and conventional skin resurfacing techniques do not work so well on rolling scars, which require processes to break up the subcutaneous fibrous bands. A GP or dermatologist will point you in the right direction.

Garden spa

Beta-hydroxy acids (BHAs) are found in the bark and the growing tips of willow trees. Some commercial remedies for scars/hyperpigmentation contain natural ingredients such as kojic derived from mushroom extract or arbutin extract, mostly from bearberry plants. An elderberry-flower wash is beneficial, but try also an elderberry mask for its replenishing and pigment-lightening ascorbic acid (or vitamin C, as we commonly know it).

Kitchen spa

Willow

Alpha-lipoic acid (ALA) is often sourced from plant or yeast extract. Alpha-hydroxy acids (AHAs) are found in strawberries, pineapple, melon, grapes and lots of other fruits. Eat them and wear them as 15-minute treatments.

ALPHA-LIPOID ACID TREATMENTS

Alpha-lipoic acid is a part of human physiology and chemistry. It is found in every cell, where its function is to turn glucose into energy, and is also antioxidant in nature. It is found in some foodstuffs too. It's a unique antioxidant in that it is not only fat- and lipid-soluble but also water-soluble, therefore reaching every part of the cell and assisting the body to rid itself of any toxins. For the purpose of acne control and treatment, its other fascinating function is in the activation of collagen-digesting enzymes that break down any damaged collagen. Damaged collagen forms the basis of scars (and also wrinkles – take note for later in life!).

Alpha-lipoic acid reduces inflammation and can arrest acne outbreaks before they develop into more seriously inflamed lesions. It is also an effective therapy for deep-pitted acne lesions because of its cell-healing properties. Alpha-lipoic acid also supports and preserves both vitamin C and vitamin E levels within skin.

ALA can be found in small quantities in peas, spinach, broccoli and other greens to boost internal reserves, but it is also found in brewer's yeast and bran to use in handy home-made face masks. Alpha-lipoic acid supplements are available, often as capsules.

Breakfast face

Put equal parts bran and oatmeal in a blender or a mortar and pestle and blitz or pound to a fine powder. Add 1 tablespoon of brewer's yeast and 1 tablespoon of honey. Mix to a paste consistency by adding a little milk, green tea or almond oil, all of which will deliver their own boost (lactic acid, polyphenols, vitamin E and vitamin K respectively). Try a different one each time.

Lunch lotion

A blitzed gloop of salad leaves and orange juice makes for a great midday cleanse and tone.

Cabbage head

The warmed leaves of cabbage (lightly steamed or dipped in hot water) have a long tradition of use as a poultice to draw out impurities from the skin.

BLUSHES, FLUSHES AND FACIAL VEINS

Spider veins, facial telangiectasia, couperose, rosacea, pityriasis rosea and tinea versicolor come under this heading.

BLUSHES

Blushing and flushing can be a reaction to weather (see *Facial spider veins* below), to a change in temperature between outside and inside, or they can be a symptom of puberty, pregnancy or menopause. Otherwise they generally occur when blood rushes to the face, ears and neck of a person experiencing a strong emotion, such as embarrassment, anger or excitement. The blush dissipates when the rush of blood dissipates.

Some people experience socially debilitating blushing, and cognitive therapy can work for them. Some people also experience sweating with the flushes and, if not due to menopause, this may be a sign of hyperhidrosis, which requires medical intervention. If it is menopause-related, sage and parsley contain phytoestrogens that limit the reaction. Continual flush is not a blush at all but a skin condition. Several skin conditions can redden the face. We will explore their specifics over the next few pages.

FACIAL SPIDER VEINS

Spider veins are generally caused by capillary frailty and the blood left behind when capillaries cannot return to normal after a flush of blood triggered by extreme temperatures or exertion. They can also be caused by hormonal changes. I recommend ginkgo tea for healthy veins. It contains beneficial antioxidants too. See also *Facial telangiectasia* below.

FACIAL TELANGIECTASIA (aka thread veins or flush blush)

Facial telangiectasia manifests as thin red or blue thread veins, i.e. your capillaries become visible just below the skin's surface. It is a condition where the capillaries can flush with blood but are slow to release that blood after exercise, a hot cup of tea, a cold brisk walk, etc. Gardeners' alfresco Cup-a-Soups in mid-winter or excess sun exposure at other times of the year can cause thread veins or exacerbate their appearance. Facial telangiectasia can also be triggered by ageing, pregnancy, oestrogen surges and also by some hereditary factors. Thyroid disorders can cause spider veins in the legs and thread veins in the face, so it might be worth a check-up to rule that out.

Facial telangiectasia can manifest as what I call a flush blush – those rosy cheeks that may last a few hours or a few weeks post exposure. Avoid washing your face in cold or hot water and moisturise after gardening to minimise flush and strengthen skin. A thicker layer of skin conceals those capillaries better and most of the facials in this book work to regenerate or reinvigorate skin.

Garden spa

I love breads and pastries with poppy seeds or sesame seeds and am forever recommending gardeners' sandwiches for different ailments. Apart from eating your garden supply, many stores stock edible seeds that are a great way of getting linoleic acid and vitamin E, which can improve peripheral vascular complaints including facial telangiectasia and couperose skin. Why not crush some seeds in a pestle and mortar with a little olive oil to make a facial treatment? Seeds that contain linoleic acid and helpful oils include blackcurrant and other ribes seeds, pumpkin, melon, watermelon, sunflower, grape, rose, evening primrose, cape gooseberry, nigella and borage.

Kitchen spa

Eating more fruit, veg and salad crops is a great way to improve capillary strength and lessen red-face issues. An old folk remedy for flush blush and other complexion issues, now a part of the Hollywood jet set's beauty treatment arsenal, is the internal and external use of apple cider vinegar with the 'mother' intact, meaning that the cloudy particles or strings remain in the bottom of the bottle. That residue is full of pectin, malic acid, numerous beneficial enzymes and trace minerals, all of which are great for digestion, internal toxin elimination and external pH and sebum balance.

Apple cider face cleanser

Topically applied, apple cider vinegar is antibacterial, antiviral and antifungal, and it removes excess oil and balances the skin's pH level. As a fruit product, apple cider vinegar naturally contains alpha-hydroxy acids, which will contribute to the exfoliation of dead skin cells and the removal of pore residue (dirt and bacteria). It kind of makes the perfect cleanser. Always do a patch test first, as sensitive skin may need a more diluted solution.

Method

This is an incremental treatment, as it can sting the first few times, especially if you have a shaving nick or an acne breakout. So for the first few times make a 1:4 ratio of apple cider vinegar to warm water. Use a tablespoon to measure out quantities; this will supply enough to dab over your face. Also, if you make it in small batches the freshness of the active ingredients is not lost. As your skin acclimatises to the apple cider vinegar, you can adjust the ratio to 1:2 or even 1:1.

Application

Once the diluted apple cider vinegar mix is made, simply dip a clean cotton-wool pad or ball into it and apply to the face with gentle upward strokes. You can use it as you would any commercial cleanser, moisturising afterwards or washing your face with warm water post-treatment. It is okay to let the solution sit on your face for a few minutes or to dab-treat specific areas.

COUPEROSE

Couperose is the term used to describe skin affected by broken or dilated capillaries, resulting in red blotches or a prolonged flushed appearance. Couperose can occur on the cheeks, nose and neck. It most often affects redheads and other pale-skinned Caucasians, those with circulation issues and those whose skin is exposed to environmental stress. Extreme weather is a common trigger for couperose skin, putting gardeners in the line of fire, but alcohol, smoking and stress can cause it too.

> ### Top tip
>
> Always wash your face and affected areas with lukewarm water. Hot or cold water will only cause blood to rush to the face, leading to even more redness.

The 3 C mask

Chamomile, cabbage rose and vitamin C all have properties that soothe skin, prompt rejuvenation and help to detox pores and capillaries.

Ingredients

- ½ cup finely chopped chamomile flowers, or the contents of 6 chamomile tea bags
- ½ cup shredded cabbage rose
- 1 cup boiling water
- 1 teaspoon powdered vitamin C, or 1 fizzy vitamin C tablet
- 1 tablespoon vegetable gelatine to thicken (optional)

Method

Boil the floral ingredients in the water for 10 minutes and then blitz the decoction in a blender with the vitamin C. If the consistency is thick enough for you, just cool the mixture and apply. If you prefer a thicker consistency, add the gelatine to the blender and blitz again. Once cooled to a temperature suitable for application to the skin, smear on and leave for 15 minutes. Rinse off with lukewarm water.

ROSACEA/ACNE ROSACEA

Rosacea is a chronic skin condition somewhat similar to couperose, often causing an acne-like appearance. It affects the cheeks, forehead, nose, chin and sometimes the eyelids. It is often considered a strain of acne. Common triggers include sun exposure, cold weather, wind battering and all the realities of the outdoors commonly faced by gardeners, but emotional stress, heavy gym workouts and hot baths can also trigger flare-ups.

Rose water toner

This is a skin rejuvenator and soothing wash for rosacea and other skin aggravations. Rose water is best produced from freshly picked petals. I like to give the rose flower a gentle hose down on the bush to remove any insects and dirt particles. There are two methods you can follow after picking the petals. The benefits of steam-distilled rose water are many, but fear not, as the steeping method yields the healing properties too. The advantage of steam-distilling is that the residue left over in the pot is actually steeped-method rose water, so you get two for the price of one.

Rose

Steeping method (infused water): Harvest some flowers and place the petals into a saucepan. Add just enough distilled/ spring water to cover the petals, or no more than twice their volume. Bring to the boil and then reduce to a simmer – we want steam but not a rolling boil. Put the lid on and allow to sit until the petals leach their colour into the water. You may notice some rose oil floating on the surface. Strain to remove the solids and decant into a clean container. Keeps in the fridge for two weeks.

Distillation method (hydrosol): (see page 35) This is a more involved process but it's worth it. The hydrosol keeps for two weeks in a fridge or longer if frozen in an ice-cube tray.

FRECKLES, SUNSPOTS AND UV DAMAGE

FRECKLES (part 1)

All I have to say on the subject is a girl without freckles is like the night sky without stars.

FRECKLES (part 2)

That was all I had to say but my publishers wish me to expand. I am Irish; I grew up playing kiss chasing with freckle-faced cailíní. To me freckles are something beautiful, wonderful and endearing. I am emotionally invested beyond nostalgia and I hate to think of a child or teenager being self-conscious about something as natural as freckles. I am proud of my own and I don't fear their return each summer. So I am all for every leopard keeping its spots just the way they are, but if you are not, read on.

Real freckles, those that form in childhood on the face, arms and other sun-exposed areas but fade in depth of colour and diminish in quantity in adulthood, are known as ephelides, an accumulation of pigmentation within the part of our skin cells known as keratinocytes. Ephelides occur and are more prominent in summer but diminish considerably or even disappear altogether in winter or during the rest of the year as skin cells turn over and new keratinocytes are formed.

In later life the freckle may be replaced by lentigines or sunspots. Perhaps the technical difference is of little concern – you just want the tip on making them fade quicker – but for now, sun protection or sun avoidance will reduce the quantity of ephelides, and eating carrots and tomatoes can help control melanin production and boost your natural SPF (sun protection factor) if you fear the freckle that much.

Garden spa

Cover up. A wide-brimmed hat that casts shade on the face prevents the sun from 'cooking up' the freckles. The juice of chamomile, parsley and lawn daisies have traditionally been used to fade freckles. They are best used at night.

Kitchen spa

Tomatoes and other foods rich in vitamin C can help inhibit the activity of tyrosinase in the skin and so reduce the formation of melanin and its accumulation. Carrots and other foods rich in provitamin A protect skin and may also have a role in naturally lightening freckles. Lemon juice is the best pigment-reducing 'friendly acid' to hand, although it works better for some than others. If you must treat your freckles, make sure to replenish the skin with some of the cellular-rejuvenating treatments listed in this book.

LENTIGINES/SUNSPOTS/AGE SPOTS/LIVER SPOTS

Lentigines are flat brown spots that appear on the face and hands, generally in middle age (hence *age spots*) but sometimes earlier. They are a result of sun damage. They are often mistaken for freckles. Like freckles they are due to a localised proliferation of melanocytes, but unlike freckles they don't disappear in the winter. There are many common names for sunspots, age spots or liver spots, but the correct term is solar lentigines (the singular is lentigo, but rarely are they experienced in the singular). Sun protection is the answer to avoiding these and to minimising them once they have occurred.

There are skin-lightening creams and treatments based on hydroquinone, which work by both decreasing the production of the melanin pigment and increasing the breakdown of melanosomes (the pigment's minute granules), effectively by disrupting the activity of tyrosinase, the enzyme needed to make melanin. But adding a little more vitamin C to your diet can do the same job. Or you can apply it topically in facials containing extra vitamins.

Elder mask (forgive the pun)

A skin mask with elderberries, orange rind and olive oil can work wonders. Put ½ cup of vitamin C-rich berries, the rind of 1 orange and 1 tablespoon of oil into a blender. Blitz and then apply. You can stir in a little honey or almond flour to create a thicker consistency if you prefer. Leave on for 15–20 minutes.

The fruit punch facial

No black eyes, just power-packing glutathione. Make your own version of a fruit mask from any combination of avocados, peaches, watermelon, cinnamon, cardamom and turmeric, topically applied in pulp-pastes to lighten pigment and boost skin health. Leave on for 15–20 minutes. The AHAs in the fruits also promote collagen and elastin renewal and the spices can boost firmness and improve the texture of skin.

UV DAMAGE

Ultraviolet (UV) damage most often presents in the chronic (long-term) form of the sunspots discussed above and in its acute (short-term or sudden-onset) form as sunburn. Limiting UV damage is all about limiting direct and unprotected exposure and maximising sun protection.

Garden spa

Prevention is better than cure, so on sunny days try to avoid sun exposure between 10 a.m. and 2 p.m. Note that the shade of a tree in full leaf can provide sun protection to the tune of SPF 10–20, but you will need more than that to shield your skin. Wear suitable protective clothing including long sleeves, sunglasses and wide-brimmed hats, and regularly apply a sun block with an SPF of at least 30.

Kitchen spa

There are foods that boost the skin's natural SPF. In particular tomatoes, red bell peppers and watermelons all share a pigment called lycopene, the role of which in plants is UV protection. In a human context lycopene has an SPF of about 3 – not a lot you may say, but that's 3 extra added on top of your sunblock. Carotenoids naturally activate human melanin and are found in carrots, beetroots and sweet potatoes. Black tea and pomegranates share some powerful polyphenol compounds that strengthen the skin's ability to protect itself against harmful UV rays. Barley, rye and oats contain tocotrienols that can alter how we absorb sunlight, filtering the harmful UV light.

Apple and apple cider vinegar mask

The pectin in apple is not only regenerative and anti-ageing but it helps build up your UVB defences. Cider vinegar tones the skin.

Ingredients

- 1 medium apple
- 2 tablespoons honey
- 3 tablespoons apple cider vinegar

Method

Quarter and core the apple, remove the pips. Put the segments in a blender with the honey and vinegar. Blitz to a paste. Apply directly to your face (or chill, if a cool mask will hit the spot). Get comfortable and relax for 15–30 minutes. Then rinse off and pat skin dry.

SUNBURN

Sunburn is a solar burn or, more specifically, the consequence of overexposure to UV radiation from the sun. It manifests as erythema (reddening) and oedema (swelling related to a build-up of fluid) and can be painful or hot to the touch. It can blister, peel and/or develop secondary infections including microscopic cellular changes that pose a cancer risk (particularly melanoma, basal cell carcinoma and squamous cell carcinoma).

In severe cases sunburn may be considered a second-degree burn. Sunburn in general can cause electrolyte imbalances, including dehydration, and can trigger neurological stress that can result in fever, chills, fainting and even circulatory shock. If you experience sunburn it is important to prevent further damage – get inside or into the shade. Rehydrate and fan areas of hot skin. A cool to lukewarm shower or bath can ease side effects but do not cool too rapidly. Leave blisters intact; if they burst on their own apply an antibacterial wash or ointment. The main treatment emphasis is to provide relief to the discomfort of the burn, generally with analgesics or aftersun moisturisers.

Garden spa

Succulents can provide cooling sap. Notably, aloe vera cools the burn, lessens the reddening and encourages skin regeneration. Many herbal teas can reduce inflammation, and those listed in this book will help with their calming influence as well as their other properties. Many can be chilled and spritzed onto hot skin for post-sun relief. Crambe and acanthus foliage can be blended with natural yoghurt or steamed and cooled to use in a poultice for their anti-itch, astringent and emollient properties.

Kitchen spa

The dairy fats in milk and yoghurts are remedial to UV-radiation damage and they are cooling too, when applied topically. Try a squeeze of lemon juice or a dash of apple cider vinegar to cool, reduce inflammation, disinfect and promote faster recovery. Pre-empting potential damage is always a good way to go. Eating about twenty almonds delivers approximately 14mg of vitamin E, which can slow the burn rate and protect your skin cells from UV light and free-radical damage.

AFTERSUN REMEDIES

Quick-fix aftersun soother

Baking soda helps to balance your skin's pH and speed recovery and healing. Black tea has tannins that reduce inflammation and promote healing. Natural yoghurt is a cooling agent and, like baking soda, works to balance the pH of skin and encourage faster healing with its natural enzymes.

Method
In a cup, moisten 2 tablespoons of black or green tea (or the contents of 2 tea bags) with 2–3 tablespoons of boiling water. Allow to stand for 1 minute and then add 2 tablespoons of baking soda. Stir in a dollop of natural yoghurt, mix well and then apply to your skin. Store in fridge for up to three days and apply often to cool and encourage healing.

Quick-fix aftersun peel-heal gel

The sap from a leaf of aloe vera mixed with 1–2 tablespoons of vinegar can slow or prevent peeling and speed recovery, with the bonus of a cooling sensation. But to boost its effectiveness you can grate some cucumber or some raw potato flesh and then blitz everything in a blender with 20 drops of lavender essential oil.

Garden aftersun lotion

In a saucepan, boil 5 finger-sized segments of washed comfrey root in ½ cup water for 20 minutes. Then turn off the heat. Add 1 tablespoon of zinc ointment, 3 tablespoons of skin-softening liquid lecithin (or 1 tablespoon of honey), 2 tablespoons of cocoa (or shea butter) and 3 tablespoons of almond oil (or olive oil). Blend everything to a pulp. Add 10 drops each of lavender, tea tree and orange (or bergamot) essential oil.

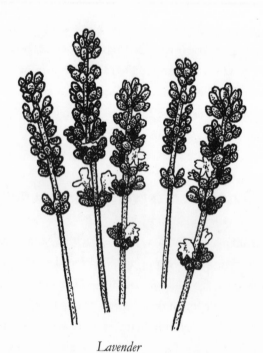

Lavender

WRINKLES

EARLY-ONSET AND AGE-RELATED

Wrinkles can begin to form as early as your twenties, especially if you have an expressive face. We gardeners are prone to that – the expression of horror at the slug damage to your row of lettuce, the puckered shock of the not-yet-ripe gooseberry, the jubilant grin when it rains in mid-July or the jaw drop of sleet the week after your tomatoes went in.

By your late twenties some may notice that those subtle laugh lines or frown lines are slower to disappear after the frown or smile is gone, and soon they can become a more regular, visible presence. Other people – the squinters – may notice faint crow's feet at the corner of their eyes first. By your thirties they will deepen and by your forties they are more accentuated. After that, deeper wrinkles are just par for the course. Or are they? The earlier you address the wrinkle issue, the less the impact will be in the future.

The sales pitch of proprietary anti-wrinkle or rejuvenation creams is usually that they contain powerful antioxidants that neutralise free-radical damage and that they are packed with vitamins and compounds that boost skin suppleness and health. Very often that means retinol (vitamin A), hydroxy acids and perhaps an ingredient such as kinetin (aka N6-furfuryladenine) to increase collagen production.

Garden spa

N6-furfuryladenine grows in your garden in all the plants mentioned in this book. It is a plant hormone responsible for cell division and for extending the longevity of plants. It is used in some commercial products to promote those actions in human skin. Plant-based poultices and compresses or creams with a botanical make-up will deliver kenetin or other cytokinins that have a similar effect. Hydroxy acids are the prime agent in fruit facials, and vitamin A is contained in topical treatments of carrot, calendula and other vitamin A-rich gardeners' staples.

Kitchen spa

Sunflower

Biotin has a role in the formation and longevity of skin cells. It is found in sunflower seeds, cheese, almonds, berries, tomatoes, onions, soya, eggs and dairy, etc. Foods rich in vitamin A help to maintain healthy cells and repair skin-tissue damage. Try carrots, sweet potatoes, red bell peppers, butternut squash, kale and romaine lettuce. Vitamin C is an antioxidant helpful in delaying wrinkle formation. Great sources of vitamin C are strawberries, watermelon, raspberries, blueberries, cranberries, cantaloupe, kiwi, pineapple and citrus fruits.

Decrease night serum

Simply mix together 1 tablespoon each of avocado oil, wheatgerm oil and calendula oil and 2 capsules each of borage seed oil (aka star oil) and evening primrose oil. One shake of lavender essential oil will boost the replenishing properties of the serum and give you a more restful sleep.

Echinacea root tea

Echinacea is an anti-inflammatory and can be used internally and topically to speed up skin regeneration or wound healing. It also contains phytonutrients that protect collagen from free-radical damage by inhibiting hyaluronidase, the enzyme that breaks down our connective tissue. Simply decoct the root in water (1 part root to 3 parts water). Strain to remove the solids and drink the 'tea'.

The snail facial

Yes, lie back and let snails crawl all over your face. I'm serious! I know gardeners have a hate/hate relationship with slugs and snails, and it's hard to ask you to get that up-close and personal with them. They are the perennial enemy after all. But if you can overcome not so much your squeamishness but your urge to crush the little molluscs, these foes might just become your friends.

The premise is that snail slime exfoliates dead cells and moisturises the newer ones beneath. It may have begun as a fad facial in Japan, but science is backing some of it up. Just as human saliva contains opiorphin – a natural painkiller six times more powerful than morphine – and thrombospondin, which helps to heal wounds, it seems snail slime has some constituents with interesting properties of their own.

Snail slime or SCA (secretions of cryptomphalus aspersa) contains a range of antioxidants that stimulate skin-cell proliferation while actively boosting skin health. The slime contains the humectant hyaluronan, similar to the hyaluronic acid used in commercial plumping and anti-wrinkle creams. In clinical trials SCA has been shown to increase skin thickness and also to decrease the signs of elastosis. The slime of the garden staple *Helix aspersa* is full of skin-rejuvenating and elastin-strengthening components such as glutamic acid, glycine and proline.

If you're going to try a snail facial, just remember that snails need to be detoxed for a couple of weeks to remove any parasites or transferable diseases, etc. The detox involves isolating them from the garden and feeding them fresh vegetables. Nobody said it would easy!

Mud masks and clay face packs

Humans have been wearing mud as long as we have been wearing animal skins (and that's long before Woodstock). As gardeners, mud is something we want to avoid; it's messy, hard to grow stuff in, needs a lot of attention, and so on. But the mud of face packs and body wraps is not wet soil; it is a mud closer to the clay used by potters. Cosmetic-grade mud is devoid of humus but is mineral rich and often enzyme rich. It is sourced from pockets in deltas, riverbanks, etc. around the world, and the location often lends a distinctive colour to the clay.

All these alluvial clays have drawing/detoxifying and germicidal actions as part of their electrical charge (see *The benefits of barefoot gardening* on page 263), but each clay type has its own unique mineral properties. Green clay, for example, is about 45 per cent silica, a mineral most beneficial to skin function and health.

MUD/CLAY TYPES SUITABLE FOR FACIAL MASKS

GREEN CLAY (aka French clay, as it is mined in France) is highly absorbent of sebum/oil and of pore-held toxins. It is a tonic and is stimulating to circulation.

RED CLAY contains more iron than other colours of clay.

YELLOW CLAY can contain more sulphur than other clays.

FULLER'S EARTH is a sedimentary clay often recommended for acne and blemishes. It has a lightening effect on skin tone and is a potent detoxifier.

RHASSOUL CLAY (aka Moroccan clay, as it is mined there) is rich in magnesium and silica. It makes a smooth paste and nourishes the skin.

BENTONITE CLAY is actually volcanic ash, traditionally used as an internal supplement to treat mineral deficiencies, but as a face mask it can perform the same task externally.

KAOLIN CLAY is found in commercial deodorants, moisturisers and some other cosmetic products. It is gentle and nourishing.

How to make a clay mask

Simply mix the clay powder and liquid to a paste of your preferred consistency. It is perhaps easier to sprinkle the powder over the liquid and build up from there. Once at the point where you think it's almost done but a tad too runny, leave it to soak for 5–10 minutes just to see how it will develop. Finally, stir well and add more liquid or powder as needed. Wear for 20–30 minutes and then rinse off.

MODIFYING A MUD MASK TO SUIT YOUR SKIN TYPE OR NEEDS

Most clay masks can be bought in powder form. The easiest way to maximise your mask is through the judicious choice of the liquid element – what you mix it with to turn it back into mud. It doesn't have to be plain water.

- Witch hazel benefits oily skin.

- Diluted honey will hydrate dry skin.

- Rose water benefits sensitive skin.

- Fruit juice adds AHA to help renew the complexion.

- Any herbal teas recommended for your skin type or issues can bring their benefits to the mask.

- Hydrosols add fragrance and the benefits of the plant they are made from.

- Egg whites are used to firm skin.

- Egg yolks are used to nourish ageing skin.

- Beer is used for the restorative action of hops and yeast.

- A cup of coffee will energise.

- Cow's milk provides extra exfoliation of dead cells.

- Asses' milk will help if your aim is to rule Egypt.

EYES, EYEBROWS
AND LASHES

They say true beauty shines from the eyes, but in this modern age our eyes are more prone to strain (refraction from computer screens, reading phone texts, hours on your tablet or watching the goggle-box) and also more susceptible to the temptation of excess (all-night wine bars, 24-hour coffee shops, movie marathons and the like). Gardeners, too, look at things a lot: is that the start of black fly? Is that drill straight? Does that colour work there? And so on. Also, we expose our eyes to more sun, dust, pollen and grit than non-gardeners, and we even occasionally rub our eyes with a sleeve or the cuff of a gardening glove to address a piece of grit or a tear.

EYES

DRY EYES
Eyebright drops and herbal infusions will soothe and resolve the problem of a dry eye, but if this is a persistent issue, add to your diet evening primrose, borage and blackcurrant seed oils. They contain the fatty acid known as gamma-linolenic acid (GLA), which supports tear production and eye hydration.

WATERY EYES

Try a cotton-pad compress of chamomile tea to soothe. A cleansing and antimicrobial fennel tea-wash is great too, in case of any underlying pathogen or complication such as a bacterial or fungal infection.

WEARY EYES

A compress of a slice of cucumber, raw potato or a strawberry will rejuvenate weary and tired eyes. The closed-eye rest for the duration of the compress does no harm either. Rose water or witch hazel compresses are excellent to soothe too.

Strawberry

SUN-SQUINT EYES

Squinting causes wrinkles, so it's a good idea to invest in good sunglasses. Also, try adding some micro-algae to your diet – not the gunk from the pond but some health-shop packets of chlorella or spirulina, which contain a particularly potent carotenoid called astaxanthin. You thought you were good giving it 110 per cent, but astaxanthin is 550 times more potent than vitamin E in protecting the eyes against ultraviolet radiation. It does the same trick for skin, so it's a win-win situation.

TIRED EYES

Puffiness, bags, dark circles, bloodshot eyes, sensitivity to light, irritation, blurred or double vision, dry or watery eyes and even pain in the neck, shoulders or back can all be signs of tired eyes.

So apart from pulling up the plants instead of weeds, tired eyes can cause the gardener other headaches.

Garden spa

Ophthalmologists may say that the majority of eye fatigue is really caused by dryness, but those of us with regular bouts know that stress and long days contribute too. The garden has a whole array of flowers that can be used in petal compresses and cooled infusions to soothe tired eyes with their beneficial phytochemicals. The humble lawn daisy, chamomile, eyebright, elderflower, cornflower, poppy, calendula and rose are all useful for this purpose. Many plants can yield a pulp or sap to use in an eye gel to soothe the area around the eye. Strawberry, apple, cucumber or aloe vera are good for this. But whether it's a rinse of the eye or a cooling of the surrounding area, the 'moment out' is a great opportunity to power down and relax. This allows our natural healing response to go to work without stress and it alleviates the agitation or the tiredness that triggered the condition.

Daisy

Kitchen spa

Whole milk, full of protein, amino acids and lactic acid, is great to reduce both eye irritation and the puffiness associated with tired eyes. Don't drink it; soak some cotton pads in it and chill them for a soothing compress that also delivers a dose of remedial vitamin A and D.

Aloe Vera, green tea and cucumber eye gel

The phytoconstituents of aloe vera sap help firm and rejuvenate the skin but also serve to lighten dark circles, decrease puffiness and soothe tension. Green tea is a great skin tonic and astringent and is also a capillary antioxidant, while the cucumber hydrates and its salt content helps with the elimination of toxins and further diminishes puffiness and discolouration.

Ingredients

- 1 small aloe vera leaf or 5 tablespoons 100 per cent pure aloe vera gel
- ¼ small cucumber
- 4–5 tablespoons green tea

Method

Slice a segment of aloe leaf and scrape out the gooey sap. Chop ¼ off a cucumber, peel it and chop the flesh. In a bowl, put 4–5 tablespoons of green tea leaves and cover with just enough boiling water to submerge. Add the other ingredients and, using a hand blender, blend until smooth. Refrigerate briefly to boost the effect. Simply dab around the eyes. Keeps in the fridge for up to two weeks.

BLOODSHOT EYES

Bloodshot eyes are the result of an inflammation of the small blood vessels on the surface of the eye. This is triggered by an insufficient supply of oxygen to the cornea, which can itself be triggered by high blood pressure, fatigue, eye strain and, of course, alcohol consumption. A lack of vitamin B2 and B6 is another possible cause. All of these are manageable and, once addressed, the problem should disappear.

Garden spa

Lutein-packed calendula flower heads are an eye tonic. Use them in a compress of mashed petals (in a drop of cold black tea) to soothe externally, and as a wonderfully refreshing herbal tea or as an additive to juices or smoothies for an internal top-up of macular vitamins.

To directly address the problem of insufficient supply of oxygen to the cornea, ginkgo tea will help boost peripheral circulation and the conveyance of both oxygen and regenerative nutrients to the eye. Purple loosestrife has traditionally been used as an eye brightener.

Kitchen spa

If you wish to, you can take a vitamin B complex supplement for a few weeks to boost your levels. It will address bloodshot eyes and all the contributing factors. But simply eating more leafy veg and salad greens will boost B vitamins and also get the retina-strengthening lutein into the bloodstream. And yes, carrots and any colourful veg with carotenoids will strengthen your eyes too.

But in the short term, a little rest works wonders and a couple of cucumber slices will soothe the eyes.

Eyebright drops/compress

Eyebright tea is excellent to revive bloodshot eyes. It goes all the way back to the earliest herbals, and both Theophrastus and Dioscorides prescribed it for ocular complaints. The traditional method is to infuse the eyebright tops in boiling water for 1 hour to extract the zinc, selenium, copper, beta-carotene and beneficial phytonutrients. Use 30g of eyebright to 500ml of water.

Eyebright

Alternatively, 1 tablespoon of eyebright tops and 1 teaspoon of chopped fennel can be infused in a cup of boiling water and then allowed to cool before straining to remove the solids. Use the remaining liquid as drops or cotton-pad compresses. Both recipes refrigerate well for three days.

Some health stores stock eyebright tea bags that can be used in the same way as an ordinary black tea bag or a chilled cucumber slice. If you don't have eyebright, fennel tea works well to detox eyes and bring brightness back.

Note: Anything you plan to put into your eyes should be made under sterile conditions.

DARK CIRCLES

Cosmetic creams containing phylloquinone (vitamin K) are often recommended as a treatment for dark circles, but the effectiveness of vitamin K really depends upon the cause of the discolouration. If the causative factor is broken capillaries, it will certainly help. If the cause is excessive alcohol consumption, not so much. Sun exposure, tobacco use, lack of sleep, allergies and hereditary factors all play a role in dark circles.

If the discolouration is bluish in tone, you are likely dealing with broken or leaky capillaries, as oxygenated blood is bluish in colour. Vitamin K promotes blood-clotting and will help heal/ seal the leak. It can take six or so weeks for the leaked blood to be reabsorbed, so it will take the dark circles a similar length of time to fade.

Garden spa

While you tackle the underlying cause of your dark circles, you can make a poultice mask of blitzed horse chestnuts and witch hazel to simultaneously soothe and reinvigorate. Both ingredients will lighten dark circles through their astringency and capillary-strengthening properties and also by slightly thickening the skin to mask those fragile capillaries while they heal. Use as a chilled mask. Avoid contact with the eye itself, applying only to the skin of the surrounding area.

Butcher's broom has a long history of use as a vasoconstrictive remedy for varicose veins, haemorrhoids and spider veins. In recent times it has found its way into cosmetic creams that address puffy eyes, black eyes and dark circles too. The astringent foliage of the shrub also contains the anti-inflammatory ruscogenin, and it can be utilised in lotions, poultices or pastes made from the pulped foliage.

Kitchen spa

Eating leafy greens full of vitamin K will help, while a blitzed kale or broccoli poultice mask is an inexpensive way to deliver phylloquinone. Those slices of cucumber that cool the eye area and tired eyes also contain vitamin C and vitamin K, two powerful antioxidants that diminish dark circles under the eyes.

Potato poultice mask

Potatoes are packed with vitamin C and many trace elements that can help resolve dark circles and address underlying causes. By all means eat a few more this week, but why not hold one back for a raw poultice mask. You make the poultice mask by peeling and grating ½ a small raw potato and blitzing it in a blender with 2 tablespoons of your favourite astringent (green tea, black tea, witch hazel). Apply and relax for 10 minutes while it works its magic. Or you can simply peel and slice a few potato circles – much as you would cucumbers – and apply to the eyes and cheeks.

EYE BAGS

These are the sagging reminders of late nights, too much work or too much recreation.

Garden spa

Rose water or witch hazel compresses are excellent to soothe. Hydrosols of clary sage, eyebright or elderflower make excellent all-round eye and skin tonics.

Kitchen spa

For eye bags, think tea bags. A cup of tea on your favourite garden seat with a tannin-rich tea bag on your eye works a treat to reduce inflammation. Chilled cucumber (the high water content rehydrates as much as the chill deflates) is a staple. Make a smoothie with plenty of vitamin C (fruit) and vitamin B (to avoid the bitter spinach element – I know some hate it – try 1 teaspoon of wheatgerm or brewer's yeast instead) to boost your system, kill the hangover (if that's what it is) and activate your natural immune system and antihistamine/anti-inflammatory responses.

Long day's eye reviver

The common lawn daisy derives its name from 'day's eye', a hint at the fact that the flowers close at night, but it also has a history as an ophthalmic herb. The flowers contain tannin and the foliage traces of calcium and magnesium. Distilled daisy-water is long recorded as a remedy for failing eyesight and inflammations of the eye, while a compress of crushed leaves and flowers is helpful in treating dark circles, black eyes and swellings. As a wash/rinse the distilled water of daisy or a strained and cooled tisane of daisy flowers is reputed in folklore to be a tonic for the eyes.

Black tea eye compress

For puffy, bagged or black eyes
Your average tea bag is packed with tannins and bioflavonoids that reduce inflammation and are a remedy for damaged blood vessels.

Method
Make a cup of tea without milk or sugar. Lift out the tea bag but do not squeeze out the excess water. Sit it on a saucer to cool. When cooled enough to be safely left on the skin, apply the wet, cool tea bag over the eye as you would with a cucumber slice and relax while it works its magic. Note that the tea bag can stain the skin around the eye for a while if you leave it on too long.

PUFFY EYES

A gentle massage in a circular motion around your eyes will reduce some puffiness by flushing blood in and toxins out. Again, a chilled tea bag will help reduce puffiness through its astringent action and cooling properties, but a cup of coffee can help too – well, more a cotton pad dipped in some cool coffee and used as an eye compress for 5 minutes or so. This will decrease puffiness and perk up your eyes too.

If puffiness is regular or constant, and not just the consequence of a late night or a reaction to an allergen, the best thing you can do is to retrain yourself to sleep right. By that I don't just mean a decent number of hours but also quality sleep. Darkening your bedroom will help immensely, and a cooler room encourages a more restful sleep. Another thing that alleviates puffy eyes is using a thick pillow or two, as keeping your head high while sleeping helps to prevent swelling around the eyes and head congestion.

Garden spa

A slightly chilled compress or other external treatment containing raspberry leaf tea is soothing and restorative. A paste of poppy and peony flowers made in a mortar and pestle is also good. Evening primrose oil is an anti-inflammatory; the flowers are edible and work from within, while the root (raw or cooked) makes a great skin-toning poultice. The anti-inflammatory ruscogenin contained in the foliage of butcher's broom is a potent vasoconstrictive remedy. Many herbal teas (chamomile, valerian, passionflower and lemon balm) will help you get a good night's sleep, while topical application of witch hazel and fennel seed tea can both soothe irritation and treat inflammation.

Kitchen spa

Splashing on or drinking cold water can cool inflammation and rehydrate. When you've had a bit too much to drink, it also addresses salt levels. Cucumber (or other chilled vegetables or fruits) used as soothing eye pads also contain astringent agents. A chilled tannin-rich tea bag is invaluable too.

Cucumber eye reviver

For puffiness, irritation and tired eyes

Cucumbers have a high water content so they chill well. The moisture and the coolness will help soothe eyes and the skin surrounding the eyes. While a chilled tea bag might do the same, cucumbers have just the right trace amounts of salt to draw excess water from the tissue surrounding the eyes, reducing the puffiness and simultaneously toning and firming the eyelids and the skin around the eyes.

Method

Thinly slice a chilled cucumber into rounds. It's better to use several thin slices rather than two thick goggles, as they will better mould to the contours of your eyes and face. Place the slices over your eyes and leave on for 5–15 minutes.

Elderflower and eyebright eye gel

The mucilage of the vegetable gelatine in this recipe nourishes the skin around the eye, while the plant parts are astringent and toning.

Ingredients

- 30ml water
- 1 teaspoon dried eyebright herb or chopped fresh leaves
- 1 head of fresh elderflowers
- 30ml witch hazel extract
- 1 teaspoon vegetable gelatine

Method

Place the water, eyebright and elderflowers in a saucepan. Cover and bring to a boil. Allow to simmer for 5 minutes and then add the witch hazel. Turn off the heat and allow to rest for 10 minutes. Strain to remove the solids. Add the vegetable gelatine and allow it to melt in the solution. Stir well and allow to set in a storage container. It will set to a consistency somewhere between wallpaper paste and hard jelly. Crush or rub between your fingers to achieve a consistency suitable for application to the skin. Refrigerates well for between a week and ten days.

COSMETIC EYES

Here are some simple remedies to pamper yourself or to prepare for a special day or night out.

Bright lights preparation

Make a simple milk thistle decoction, or you can buy a supplement from a health shop. Working under bright lights or being exposed to glare in the polytunnel can cause squinting and eye strain. All the fat-soluble vitamins (A, D, E) that protect the retina and the antioxidant glutathione are stored in the liver, and the vision-boosting and light-desensitising B vitamins are activated in the liver. Milk thistle can unleash those health agents while detoxing the liver, which also promotes radiant eyes.

Eye brightener

Witch hazel extract, eyebright infusion and fennel seed tea can be used to make traditional drops or eyebaths to perk up eyes. Consuming brewer's yeast, milk thistle and orange or red foods will allow vitamins beneficial to the retina to get to where they need to go.

LATE-NIGHT EYES

One way to reduce eye fatigue caused by late nights is to improve night vision by helping eyes transition better as they adapt to the dark and back again to light. It takes the pressure off and prevents the telltale signs of strain. Purple pigmented fruits are full of anthocyanin, which helps speed up adaptation. The purple plant pigment actually accelerates the regeneration of rhodopsin, the human cellular pigment (also purple) used by the eyes' rods. So yum yum to a regular intake of bilberry, blueberry and blackcurrant, or at least for a few days before a night on the tiles and, if needs be, for a breakfast recovery.

EYEBROWS

Eyebrow conditioner

Coconut oil makes an excellent eyebrow conditioner. It can be set with beeswax to make a salve that styles and conditions.

Eyebrow enrichment mask

Mix 1 tablespoon of brewer's yeast with 1 of tablespoon castor oil and 1 tablespoon of jasmine or other petal-infused oil. Stir well. Leave on your eyebrows for 30 minutes. Rinse off with warm green tea.

EYELASHES

Lost eyelash replenisher

Green tea compresses can stimulate hair growth and help to both lengthen and clean lashes. You can also use cool cucumber slices as the chill calms tiredness and inflammation and the silicon and sulphur content will stimulate hair growth.

Eyelash volumiser

A week of applying castor oil to the base of your eyelashes at night will not only hydrate but also strengthen the lashes. The combination of the plumped-up effect of moisture and their enhanced ability to resist breakage will leave you with fuller, longer lashes. Use a cotton bud or a clean mascara brush to apply as you would mascara. Avoid getting the castor oil into the eyes. The night-time application just gives the oil longer to soak into the lashes. Rinse off in the morning.

Eyelashes have a life cycle of just a few weeks, so to maintain the effect you will need to build this trick into your routine.

MAKE-UP REMOVERS

Make-up remover

Jojoba oil, olive oil and the oil-based salves and lotions in this book can all remove make-up without resorting to moisture-stripping alcohols or additives. Coconut oil is particularly effective as it dissolves stubborn grease paint and gentle concealer with equal ease, leaving your skin moisturised in the process.

Eye make-up remover

Equal parts olive oil and witch hazel will remove eye shadow, eyeliner and mascara. Full-fat milk on a cotton pad is also effective.

Stubborn mascara remover

Avocado oil on a cotton pad makes a gentle but effective cleanser that also replenishes the lash. Mix 3 tablespoons avocado oil with 1 tablespoon castor oil. This will remove those cheap mascaras and lift the residue from thick lash products.

LIPS, MOUTH
AND TEETH

LIPCARE

One could say that the lips say it all. They are the focus point in conversation; they are an animate part of the face when we interact, not only in speech but in creating the expressions that convey our emotions. They are also alluring – the pout, the lick of the lips, the provocative bite or curl, the plumpness, the sheen, the kiss. If they weren't so important, would lipstick, lip balm, lip gloss, etc. crowd the shelves of pharmacies and supermarkets?

Lips comprise very thin layers of hairless skin and have some unusual properties. They have no sweat glands, no sebaceous glands and are also devoid of the skin hormone melanin – the body's natural defence to sun and UV damage. As a result lips do not tan but instead burn repeatedly, so they need more attention than the face or back of the neck when it comes to gardening during the summer months. The thinness of the skin on the lips and the propensity for UV damage can result in harm to the collagen and so speed up ageing and the formation of wrinkles. The lips can also lose moisture quickly, and licking your lips does more harm than good, so a good lip balm is essential, better still if it has a high SPF.

Apart from sunburn and skin cancer, overexposure to sunshine can trigger a breakout of cold sores (see page 182). The best thing you can do is use sunblock. But during the summer also plump up with an evening or night-time rub of vitamin E. Use the contents of a vitamin E capsule or olive oil, which also contains oleic acid that acts to increase the skin's moisture-retentiveness. Make a salve with vitamin E-rich sunflower oil and antiseptic and soothing beeswax. You can also use the antioxidant-rich and healing petals of calendula, rose or borage.

Lips can lose moisture quickly at any time of the year, so hydration is always key.

INFLAMED LIPS/CHEILITIS

Cheilitis is the medical term used to describe inflamed lips, whether the inflammation is caused by infection, a skin condition, an allergy, environmental factors, medication or injury, including over-licking, sunburn or severe dehydration. The inflammation of lips can develop into severe chapping, crusting and even bleeding sores if not treated appropriately.

Essential medicated lip balm

This balm is soothing and remedial to all conditions listed in this section.

The vegetable butter in this recipe is moisturising, the calendula oil is soothing and protective and the beeswax is a natural antibacterial agent that also plumps the lips. The addition of a few drops of essential oil can really boost the balm to a whole other level, as most essential oils have antibacterial, antifungal, and antiviral properties. Lip-friendly essential oils include lavender, German chamomile, tea tree, lemon, lemon thyme, sandalwood, peppermint, rose and geranium. Experiment to find a flavour or tingle that suits you.

Ingredients
- 1 tablespoon shea butter or cocoa butter
- 1 tablespoon grated beeswax
- 1 tablespoon calendula oil
- 6 shakes of your favourite essential oil

Method
In a bain-marie (or jam jar resting in hot water), melt the shea butter/cocoa butter and beeswax into the calendula oil. Once melted, remove from the heat and stir with a chopstick or just swirl around. Add the essential oil at the last minute. Decant into a suitable container such as a small glass jar or tin. Cover to retain the volatile oils. Allow to cool and set naturally. Store in a cool place and use as often as you need.

CHAPPED LIPS/CHEILITIS SIMPLEX
Chapping, be it of the hands or lips, is the bane of gardeners' lives. The problem is that the factors that trigger chapping are Clause 1 in the gardener's contract: You agree to be exposed to cold, wind, rain, hail, sun, summer heat and dry air, not to mention dirt, dust, sand and, of course, dehydration. If you are in the habit of repeatedly licking your lips as you flick through a

seed catalogue or favourite gardening magazine, that won't help either.

Let's face it, chapped lips are just not as appealing as a well-hydrated kisser, but beyond the aesthetic, dry, cracked lips (medically referred to as cheilitis simplex) can soon become sore lips and complicate day-to-day activities such as eating, shouting at pigeons, phoning the meteorological office to order some sunshine, smiling, wincing or kissing that prized packet of seeds that just arrived in the post, never mind the postman who delivered it.

Top tip

Resist repeatedly licking your lips. Saliva evaporates quickly and can leave your lips even drier than before. Instead apply a balm or home-made seal and drink plenty of fluids to keep yourself and your lips and the rest of your skin hydrated while working outside. Avoid citrus juice and fruits, as they aggravate chapped lips.

Garden spa

Many commercial balms and lipsticks contain alcohol and/or petroleum products, which can aggravate chapped lips rather than help them, especially if your dry lips are related to medication, allergens or environmental stresses. Natural products are best. Try the hydrating and skin-replenishing sap of aloe vera, or make a pulp of cucumber flesh for the same effect. Rose has a natural affinity with skin and also with the skin of lips. You can make a salve or balm with home-made rose oil.

Kitchen spa

A smear of olive oil will hydrate and soothe chapped lips. A smear of honey is great, as apart from its moisturising properties, it functions as an antiseptic. A mix of oil and honey with a few added sugar grains can exfoliate the dry skin and soothe the exposed new skin. If you are going out to smell roses or venturing near bees, perhaps leave the honey out!

Thistle tea

Chapped lips can be the result of an underlying condition. Creeping thistle, cited in old American herbals and sometimes sold in health shops as extract of Canadian thistle, or botanically as *Cirsium arvense*, is currently being investigated as a natural antibiotic to replace our dwindling pharmacological options. One of its oldest ethnobotanical uses is to treat skin eruptions and skin ulcers, and certainly its efficacy as a treatment for chapped lips and hands has long been part of gardeners' lore. In conventional medicine some cases of chapped lips that become infected are treated with antibiotics.

Method

Simply make a decoction by boiling a few creeping thistle leaves in water for 20–30 minutes (a ratio I like is 20g chopped and pounded leaf to 100ml water). Strain to remove the solids and store in the fridge for up to one week. Use as a lip wash three times daily for the week.

Essential rose and honey lip balm

Both the rose and the honey in this recipe are healing to chapped skin and the flavour they impart is exquisite.

Method

In a bain-marie, melt 2 teaspoons of grated beeswax into 3 tablespoons of sweet almond oil. Once the wax has dissolved, stir in 1 tablespoon of honey and remove from the heat. Add 10–20 drops of rose essential oil to boost fragrance and healing potential. Decant into small glass or metal storage containers. This stores well for months in the pocket of overalls, in the shed drawer or in your handbag. Use regularly to remedy and prevent recurrence.

Sun-infused rose petal balm

This is made in the same way as the balm above, but with a handful or two of rose petals left to infuse in the bottle of almond oil for a few weeks before making the remedy. This rose oil will give a boost to the tonic value of the balm.

COLD SORE/HERPES SIMPLEX LABIALIS

A cold sore manifests as a small blister or cluster of blisters occurring on the lips (and sometimes also the face). It is caused by a viral infection called herpes simplex virus type 1 (HSV1). Tingling, itching or burning sensations generally herald the blistering to come. It is highly contagious and it has its own lifecycle. Some people get a cold sore once and it never returns but with most, once contracted, the virus remains with you for many years if not forever. Thankfully it is normally dormant, with possibly one or two flare-ups each year, but it is also easily triggered into activity by sunburn or other damage to the lips' surface and also by stress or fatigue. So looking after yourself is the best way to keep it suppressed.

Outbreaks generally clear up without any intervention or treatment within seven to ten days. There are plenty of over-the-counter lip balms and topical creams that fight the virus and soothe the soreness, and there are also lots of home cures that make an outbreak more manageable.

Top tip

Gorse bushes bloom year round, hence the saying *When gorse is out of blossom, kissing is out of fashion*, but whether the hills are clothed in yellow or not, give kissing a miss until lips have fully recovered. A hydrosol or floral essence of gorse on the lips or in your morning juice is good to temper stress and anxiety, be it anxiety at not being able to kiss or the stress that triggered the cold sore in the first place!

Garden spa

To keep lips hydrated and to address the flare-up try antiviral iced teas made from ingredients harvested from your garden. These will not only boost your immune system but will also work topically on the lips and mouth. I would opt for chamomile as it contains bisabolol, an antimicrobial wound healer. You can also try lemon balm, bergamot, mint, echinacea and thyme. Liquorice root contains glycyrrhizic acid that can inhibit and fight the spread of the virus. Traditionally, tincture or tisane rinses of self-heal and hyssop tea or syrup are antiviral.

Kitchen spa

Avoid acidic or salty foods as they not only sting but can suppress your immune system while it's trying to fight the virus flare-up. The mistake is to eat and drink less for fear of bursting a blister or cracking a scab, but you should drink plenty of fluids to keep the lips hydrated and functioning as normally as possible.

LIP BEAUTY

Here are some helpful recipes for the perfect pout or at least a more salubrious smacker. Yes, *salubrious smacker* – when it comes to lips I go a bit 1940s! Got a problem, dollface? It's the 'just put them together and blow' thing (forgive the paraphrasing and the following nerdy reference to the same film). So if you have not, here's how to have.

Top tip

While we remember that lips should be moisturised, we may neglect to exfoliate. If you have a spare toothbrush you can gently brush your lips every now and then with a paste of honey and baking soda. The fact that you use a toothbrush every day may remind you to do it more often.

Kiss-perfect lip mask

Mash up some ripe papaya and smear over lips and upper lip. Leave for 15 minutes and then rinse. Papaya not only contains exfoliating enzymes but also phytonutrients to soften skin and lips. It also acts to refine lip lines and plump a little.

Hey sugar lip scrub

Mix together 1 teaspoon each of brown sugar and sunflower oil and use as a lip-surface exfoliator. The grains of sugar provide the exfoliating action while the sunflower oil imparts vitamins A, E and K.

Oh you salty dog you

The same as the *Hey sugar lip scrub* above but with sea salt instead of brown sugar.

Honey drip mask

Smear some honey on your lips and go as long as you can without licking it off. Try to get to at least 5 minutes. The slightly acidic pH of honey destroys bacteria and helps to regenerate the surface of the lips, while its hydrating properties soak in and plump.

Its antioxidant constituents mop up free radicals and leave lips looking younger.

> ### *Top tip*
>
> The darker the honey, the higher the content and potency of antioxidants.

Fuller-lip lotion

As we age, we experience collagen loss, which apart from its impact on the skin, also contributes to lip shrinkage. Commercial creams and lotions that claim to stimulate collagen all do so via their peptide content. These chains of up to fifty amino acids make proteins, including some for your lips. Cow's and goat's milk are rich sources of peptides. Get them in yoghurt form and mix with equal parts rose water and glycerine for a plumping treatment. To extend shelf life and use as an overnight treatment, make into a cream by adding to an oil-and-wax mixture. Simply warm up equal quantities of oil (sunflower, borage and almond are excellent) and emulsifying wax, before adding to the yoghurt mixture and blending. Keeps in the fridge for one week.

TEETH

Your smile may be your biggest asset and a pearly-white flash of teeth is reassuring (to witness and to have). But personally I am not a fan of teeth bleached so artificially white that a smile is like a welder's flash and my corneas take a week to recover. That said, a yellow grin is off-putting and can also be debilitating to personal confidence. But a great smile can be found along the garden path, not up it. If we can resist the pressure to match the airbrushed perfection offered by chemical cosmetics, there are many natural answers to a whiter, brighter smile.

Good hygiene and tooth cleaning may not mean you need to brush more. It might be more a case of when you brush. You would think it's good to brush after those foods and beverages that contribute to staining, but you could be doing more harm than good (the food acids will have slightly softened your enamel layer and make it susceptible to friction damage – wait a while). In terms of foodstuffs, just as there are those that stain, there are those that lift stains and those that contribute directly to tooth health and structure, including enamel protectors and post-meal deacidifiers. There are many foods and herbs that can be grown to improve your tooth health and its ability to resist staining.

HOW TEETH BECOME YELLOW

There are three reasons why teeth can turn from white to yellow over time. The first and perhaps best-known cause is staining from cigarette smoking, wine/coffee drinking and munching on a whole array of foods that discolour teeth. The second is the acidity of some foods and beverages, which wears away the protective white enamel coating. This is acid erosion and it reveals the yellower inner layer of dentin. Finally, tooth enamel naturally becomes more transparent with age and so reveals more of the dentin. Eating right can delay the enamel changes and also cut out the other two causes.

THE MOST ANCIENT METHOD OF TOOTH WHITENING

Fire may have revolutionised the life of primitive man, but some of its by-product may have civilised our look. It is believed that ancient man first utilised ground chalk, crushed rock minerals, white clay, ashes and even charcoal as a mouth and tooth cleanser. It seems counter-intuitive but there just may have been some method to this apparent madness.

Bright sparks charcoal mouth powder

Modern research has shown that activated charcoal placed in the mouth alters the pH balance and thus the health of the mouth, helping to eliminate the bad bacteria associated with tooth decay, combating gingivitis and also slowing cavity formation. Activated charcoal can draw toxins from the gums too.

Method

With a mortar and pestle grind some charcoal to a fine powder. Dip a clean toothbrush into the powdered charcoal, moisten your teeth with saliva and simply brush using gentle circular motions. Your mouth and teeth will go black at first, but after rinsing, the whitening effect is noticeable. Your teeth and your whole mouth will feel remarkably clean but there might be some residual taste. Give it 10 minutes and then brush with your regular toothpaste or rinse with a proprietary or home-made mouthwash.

Note: Like any whitening treatment this is not to be done daily. Overuse can undermine the enamel. No more than twice a week, or in advance of a wedding or other social function.

Top tip

Choose natural charcoal (from wood or coconut sources), which can be found in health stores, and not petroleum-based charcoal (often used in artists' and barbecue charcoal).

Strawberry whitening

The fruit acids contained in strawberries, not least malic acid, act as powerful tooth whiteners by lifting stubborn stains off the surface of tooth enamel. Many fruits have these acids, including apples, grapes, etc., but strawberries are also packed with vitamin C, which actively clears away plaque. So strawberries offer a double hit of delicious dentistry. They are also easily grown at home in a window box or hanging basket if space is limited.

METHOD 1: Eat a few strawberries at the close of a meal or for breakfast.

METHOD 2: Simply slice a strawberry and rub it over your teeth.

METHOD 3: Mash up or purée some strawberries (with a little salt or bicarbonate of soda if you like) and use as a toothpaste.

Top tip

Fruit acids are still acids, and you want to stop the acidic action after it has done its good but before it begins to erode tooth enamel. So after using a strawberry treatment, wait 15–20 minutes and then rinse with a salty solution or have a drink of milk to neutralise the fruit acids. Remember, too, that this treatment is not for everyday use over extended periods but rather as a booster when called for.

MOUTHWASHES

Garden tea total clean rinse

The menthol in the mint refreshes the mouth while sterilising the gums and killing bacteria stuck to your teeth. Thyme is an antiseptic and is soothing too. Rosemary has the qualities of both of these and is also a source of trace calcium and other minerals that benefit teeth.

Ingredients
- handful of mint leaves
- sprig of thyme
- sprig of rosemary

Method

Make a pot of tea with the herbs and allow to cool. Strain to remove the solids and decant into a jar or bottle. Rinse and gargle as needed. This keeps for several weeks in the fridge.

> ### Top tip
>
> A tincture can also be made (the same quantities of herbs as in the mouthwash recipe to 100ml vodka) and diluted 1 part tincture to 5 parts water. This way you can have a supply through the winter.

Quick-fix salty rinse

References to the treatment of gum disease and tooth decay with saltwater appear as early as 2700 BC in China's great healing systems and later in Greek and Roman *materia medica*. Salt is a natural disinfectant and it kills the bacteria responsible for tooth decay and bad breath. It is also an anti-inflammatory and is somewhat analgesic to tooth pain. Salty water is acidic, however, and should not be used daily.

Method

Simply dissolve 2 tablespoons of sea salt (table salt can be used as a substitute if necessary) in a glass of water (some tap water is fluoridated; some spring waters have calcium and other mineral traces that are beneficial to teeth) and rinse with the solution.

NECK AND DÉCOLLETAGE, CLEAVAGE AND BREASTS

NECK AND DÉCOLLETAGE

Other than the face, wrinkles are most prominent on the neck area due to the thinness of skin and paucity of underlying fatty tissue. The thinner skin of the décolletage can crinkle, or crêpe, with age and UV damage. Both areas can be prone to sunburn and other consequences of exposure to the elements. Neck and décolletage can be treated the same. Men can use the treatments here just for the neck.

Décolletage here refers to the front neckline and to the cleavage/chest. Elsewhere it can often include any area exposed by an open neckline, which, depending on the garment, could bring shoulders and back into play.

Garden spa

Pick some parsley and plaster it on. The amount of skin-replenishing vitamin C in parsley is four times higher than that in oranges. Parsley compresses also have the benefit of magnesium, calcium, phosphorus, potassium, sulphur, iodine and trace copper. The chlorophyll encourages cellular repair. Borage and evening primrose flowers make excellent petal moisturisers and their seed oil is great for rejuvenating skin. Elderflower can fade age spots, soothe sunburn and also decrease the appearance of wrinkles, so it makes a great ingredient for any 'neck and dec' treatment. Lady's mantle helps prevent skin from sagging. Both purple and yellow loosestrife make good skin treatments. Once the seeds are removed, hawthorn berries are edible, and with their pectin content, they cook up nicely with other fruit to make jams and preserves. The phytochemicals found in hawthorn and its pectin support the production and functioning of collagen.

Kitchen spa

An apple a day! Free radicals prematurely age our skin, but vitamin C in citrus fruits can mop up those free radicals. Apples can also prevent dry, flaky skin through their juicy hydration. Their pectin, vitamin A and calcium content also help skin to regenerate. Eat more apples, but also pulp up a fruit mask to get all of those benefits from an external treatment. Green and white tea inhibit collagenase and elastase from destroying collagen and elastin. Grape, fig and passion fruit make great 20-minute masks for neck and dec.

White tea and parsley décolletage gel

In a blender blitz together the contents of 1 white tea bag with ½ cup of boiling water, 1 teaspoon of vegetable gelatine, and ½ cup of parsley. Allow to cool enough to apply to crêpey areas. Use immediately as this does not store.

Peppermint and sage toner

Peppermint is an astringent in its own right and can be soaked in or blended with witch hazel to tighten skin. You can add sage to cleanse and tighten pores.

Pectin neck and décolletage mask

The pith in the rind of a lemon is packed with skin-tightening pectin, and the polysaccharides in apples can slow changes to skin structure associated with UV damage and ageing. Peel, core, dice and cook an apple with ½ a chopped lemon in 1 cup of boiling water. Blitz them in a blender and allow to cool before applying to skin. The lemon juice in the mix also supplies extra vitamin C.

Milk and two sugars cleansing milk

Cow's and goat's milk are packed with cytokines (listed on expensive creams as peptides) that lift dead skin cells and repair tissue damage underneath while also stimulating the production of collagen and other connective tissues, basically restructuring the skin so that it looks healthier and younger. In a blender, simply whip up 1 cup of milk with 5 tablespoons of sunflower oil, 2 tablespoons of almond flour, 1 tablespoon of honey and 1 tablespoon of glycerine. Stores in the fridge for one week. The oil will separate, so shake well before use. Use as a cleanser or add more almond flour for a mask consistency.

CLEAVAGE AND BREASTS

The main issue here is sagging or loss of firmness. Age, pregnancy and breastfeeding will all have an impact. It is slightly more difficult to shape and tone breasts as they are made less of muscle and more of fat, tissue and milk-producing glands, but it is possible to shape and tone the muscles around your breasts to delay sagging and create an appearance of firmness.

Garden spa

Take up garden yoga (see *The benefits of barefoot gardening* on page 263). There are many yoga poses that simultaneously help to tighten the upper chest muscles and also tone/shape the breasts. Try practising postures such as the uttanasana (standing forward bend), utthita trikonasana (triangle pose), and bhujangasana (cobra pose) to achieve firmer and more uplifted breasts.

Cobra pose

If you're not so limber, don't despair, as massage stimulates muscle growth, cellular repair and strengthening of tissue, and just like yoga, it can reduce the appearance of sagging breasts and keep taut ones taut for longer. Olive oil is firming and many garden herbs can be added to the oil to firm, retexture and combat stretch marks (see page 217).

Kitchen spa

Sticking with massage, and without going all fifty shades, you can try an ice massage. Regular one-minute bouts of circular motions with ice wrapped in a cloth is one of those supermodel secrets.

Lady's mantle lotion

The astringent properties of a decoction of lady's mantle (using foliage and roots) are firming to the décolletage and breasts. This can be easily adapted to create a lotion by decocting in milk and thickening with almond flour or gelatine, or you can use it as the base for oil-and-wax lotions (amend any in this book).

Lady's mantle

Rejuvenating hydration oil

In a small bowl, mix together 1 teaspoon each of wheatgerm oil, calendula oil and peach kernel oil. Add 5 shakes of geranium essential oil or an essential oil with a fragrance you like but that is also beneficial to skin (see page 213) and stir. Use like a massage oil.

BODY

BODY SKIN

Skin is skin, you might think, but body skin has fewer sebaceous glands than face skin and is less exposed to UV and the elements than face, neck or arm skin, unless you enjoy naturism as well as nature. Body skin is less likely to be oily but can still be susceptible to acne and pimples. It has a tendency to be dry, and the relevant treatments in the 'Face' section apply for this. That dryness combined with the covered-up nature of body skin slows down skin-cell turnover, which, while creating thicker skin, can also cause scaliness. Scaly skin may encourage bacteria, hence pimples, acne, etc.

THE THING WITH SKIN

On a very technical level, skin protects you from the environment while helping to control your body temperature. It has a role in ensuring fluid/electrolyte balance and in the elimination of toxins. But it has nerve receptors that guide us through life and make it a glorious experience. It allows us to feel sensations such as the warmth of the sun, the cooling breeze, the sweet baptism of summer rain and the chilled air of January, not to mention touch, pain and pleasure.

Skin has many layers, but we generally refer to three distinct strata: the epidermis is the outer layer, holding pigments and proteins; the middle layer is the dermis, which is home to oil glands, hair follicles, blood vessels and nerves; finally, there is the subcutis, or subcutaneous, layer with more blood vessels and also your sweat glands and fat deposits. Between each layer there are connective tissues laced with collagen fibres (providing support) and elastin fibres (providing flexibility and extra strength).

Negative changes in the skin can be due to environmental factors, nutrition and also genetic make-up, but positive changes can be achieved through care, treatment and good nutrition. Care and treatments for the different skin types (dry, oily, sensitive, etc.) are dealt with on pages 105–20, while treatments for skin conditions are best located through the index at the back of the book.

SKIN AS AN ORGAN

Your skin is your body's largest organ. I know you may have heard that before, but did you really hear it? You wouldn't put your heart, lungs or liver through the stresses that your skin endures. Thinking of it as an organ – as vital to life – may encourage you to give it some extra care. Here are things we can do to keep it healthy:

Stay hydrated. Water is essential to the functioning of your skin. A spritz or two on the outside is as helpful as a few sips of water working from the inside.

Cleanse your skin not just of dirt and grime, but of toxins too (see *Natural bath additives* on page 231) and also of dead skin cells by exfoliating at least once a week (see *Natural exfoliants* on page 226).

Lower the temperature of the shower or bath. Don't parboil yourself into premature ageing.

Moisturise before you see the need for it. It's too late when it dries – then you're just reacting to a problem instead of preventing one.

Kick the junk food, including store-bought highly processed foods.

Pick up more **fresh fruits and vegetables**. And eat them! In this book I recommend wearing a lot of them too, but, really, do eat them. We evolved to take our nutrients from fresh food. You will see a real return if you return to that practice!

Get active. Skin health depends upon good circulation. Walk, run, cycle, mow the lawn.

Get some rest. Skin benefits from a minimum of six hours of sleep (preferably at night).

Use the day. Sunshine provides skin-health vitamins.

Keep using the day. Fresh air is an opportunity to get oxygen in and clean our blood, which in turn cleans away our accumulated toxins.

When using the day, apply **a broad-spectrum sunblock** to protect uncovered skin from UV damage.

Go skinny dipping once in a while; it reminds you how fabulous you are … or makes you remember to do some of the things in this list to get fabulous for next time!

COMMON SKIN PROBLEMS

DRYNESS (see also Dry skin on page 108)

Rose and calendula skin cream

Ingredients
- 150ml calendula oil
- 90g coconut oil
- 30g emulsifying wax
- 30g cocoa butter
- 150ml rose water

Method

Warm the oils in a bain-marie. Add the wax and butter and continue to heat until fully melted. Remove from the heat and slowly add the rose water, whisking as you go. Allow to cool for 20 minutes and then whisk again. Stores well.

RASH

It's always important to find the underlying cause of a rash, but sometimes it is simply an allergic reaction to a substance, be that pollen, foliage or a new washing detergent or fabric softener.

Chamomile milk and honey lotion

All the ingredients in this lotion work to reduce inflammation and neutralise the histamine or defence reaction that occurs in nettle rash, nettle sting, heat rash, sunburn and other irritations that trigger rashes. Zinc is antipruritic (i.e. it stops itching).

Ingredients
- ½ cup chamomile flowers/tops
- ½ cup coconut or almond milk
- ½ cup strong chamomile tea
- 2 tablespoons zinc ointment or a crushed zinc tablet
- 2 tablespoons baking soda
- 2 tablespoons honey

Method
Soak the chamomile flowers in the milk overnight. Strain out the flowers and then put all the remaining ingredients in a bowl with the milk and whisk well (if using a hand blender you can leave the flowers in). Apply as needed to the affected area of skin. Keep refrigerated and use within five days of making.

Garden spa

There are many garden plants and weeds that have antihistamine properties, not least nettles, which as a foliage tea or in a culinary dish will introduce the active ingredient to the bloodstream. Washing with a cooled infusion can help a rash clear up quicker. Likewise, yarrow, basil, chamomile, echinacea, fennel, oregano and tarragon can all be ingested or directly applied to rashes and clusters of hives. A rub of aloe vera, houseleek sap, pineapple juice or burdock sap, and foliage poultices made with strawberry, myrtle, elder or green tea all work wonders too.

WARTS

Warts are a sign of a virus called the human papillomavirus (HPV), which causes the body to produce an excess of skin cells. The best way to tackle them is to attack the virus by boosting your immune system. Diet, herbal teas and vitamin supplements will all help. Warts are not just unsightly, they're also easily spread around your own body and quite contagious to others. Scratching a wart and then rubbing another skin surface can move the virus-filled cells around like seeds. In fact common warts are often referred to as seed warts.

While most warts are painless, they are ugly and some can become uncomfortable and sore, especially on the fingers and thumbs kept busy with gardening chores. Much like botrytis on tomato plants, they enter the system via cuts and nicks, often in moist areas of skin, so going from bare feet to work boots or from bare hands to sweaty gloves can provide the right conditions for incubation. Most warts will eventually resolve themselves, even without treatment, but it can take up to two years. That's two years of spreading potential, so just like a weed, once spotted, best eradicated.

Garden spa

The best way to treat warts is to tackle the virus, so immunity-boosting herbs (echinacea, thyme, astragalus) will help your system reboot and go on the attack. People with compromised immune systems or who are fatigued are more prone to warts, so some energy smoothies, along with alternative or conventional treatments, will treat the underlying cause too.

In global ethnobotany, both wild and garden-grown Euphorbia (along with other members of the spurge family) have been employed to burn off warts and other skin growths, through dabs of their caustic milky sap. Similarly dandelion milk, the corroding milky sap, was once traditionally applied two to three times daily until the wart was eradicated. Celandine was also used in this manner. There are of course gentler garden options: a petal poultice of calendula (rich in vitamin A) can soften warts to enable them to be removed with a pumice stone. Many commercial treatments echo the ancient willow sap treatment by including salicylic acid in their ingredients. Extract your own salicylic acid by blending some growing tips and foliage of willow in a little water or witch hazel extract. Apply twice daily until the wart shrinks away to nothing. This method is helped along by some post-soak work with a pumice stone.

Kitchen spa

Retinoid cream (derived from vitamin A) is used in salons or prescribed by a GP and can be quite effective at arresting the growth of warts. Vitamin A disrupts the wart's cellular development and can easily be sourced from capsule supplements as much as expensive creams. Home-pressed pumpkin seeds and apricot kernel oil are other good sources.

Radar juice/wart drops

The acidity of both lemon juice and apple cider vinegar provides some gentle corrosive action and cellular alteration that forces our own immune system to find the blip and deal with it. The vitamin C content in the fruit juice is also beneficial to skin recovery after the wart has been eradicated, as well as contributing to the destruction of the virus that causes the wart. Use in compresses, corn plasters or as topical drops.

BODY ACNE

Body acne is no different from facial acne, but it is best treated with body washes, baths (see page 230), cleansers and exfoliants that incorporate salicylic acid (see page 229) or glycolic acid (see page 227). Willow and Epsom salts make great bath additives. Thyme and avocado make a great body wash. (See also *Scars* on page 214.)

Love, not war bath salts

Acne can be a difficult journey. Puberty and hormonal fluxes that contribute to acne can be an emotional roller coaster, and the two combined can be seriously stressful. The shocking thing – the Catch 22 of it – is that stress aggravates acne flare-ups and acne flare-ups increase stress levels. Worry alone can trigger inflammation and oxidative stress. Anxiety raises unhelpful cortisol in the bloodstream while simultaneously depleting reserves of zinc, selenium and magnesium, the very minerals that help us fight acne. So loving yourself with a pampering lavender and Epsom salt bath can reduce stress levels and boost some of those depleted minerals and other nutrients, as well as phytochemicals, to collectively calm an outbreak. Win-win!

Ingredients

- 2 cups Epsom salts
- 1 cup baking soda
- ½ cup sea salt
- ½ cup lavender flowers
- 21 drops of essential oil of lavender
- food colouring (optional)

You will also need

- 1 Ziploc bag or resealable freezer bag
- 1 sheet baking parchment/wax paper
- 1 mason jar or other container

Method

Put all the dry ingredients in the Ziploc bag. Seal and shake well. Add 7 drops of essential oil of lavender. A drop of food colouring added at this stage can add a ripple of colour to the salts. Seal again and shake. Repeat three times, adding a further 7 drops of essential oil each time. Spread the salts out onto the wax paper/baking sheet and allow to air dry for approximately 1 hour. Stir after about 30 minutes. Store in airtight containers. Use as required. About a tablespoon is enough for a bath.

BODY SPOTS AND PIMPLES

Spots and pimples are extensively covered in the facial skin section (see page 128) but also take a look at exfoliants (page 226) and bath additives (page 231). The expressed resin and bark of ivy is also a traditional antiseptic for boils (you can blitz the stems and bark together), and heated-leaf poultices address body pimples. Do a patch test before treating, as some people are sensitive to ivy.

BOILS/FURUNCLES

Once a biblical plague, a boil or furuncle is simply a hair follicle infected by the bacteria *Staphylococcus aureus*. Often thought of as an infected pimple, they can begin like pimples – red and inflamed – but the follicle swells well beyond pimple size to become a painful lump, often 1.5cm in diameter, filling with pus and later bursting (or requiring lancing). A yellow or white head can manifest at the centre of the lump when the boil is ready to discharge its pus. You may need a GP or dermatologist to drain a boil if it does not burst of its own accord or if it becomes excessively painful. Most boils have a life span of two weeks, but some are more persistent. Boils can arise on any part of the body where hair follicles are present but predominantly appear on the face and neck, in the underarm area, on the back and chest, the groin, thighs and buttocks and also occasionally on the scalp and inner ear canal. Men are more prone to boils. A cluster of boils is known as a carbuncle.

Garden spa

Old herbal remedies often recommend infusions of curled/yellow dock or milk thistle to eliminate toxins, but because the toxins flush to the skin, I would rather use a compress of steamed dock leaf to draw out the pus, or else use pastes of burdock, heartsease, chickweed or yarrow, which are also remedial. Taking in echinacea is good to bump up the immune system. An astringent and antibiotic infusion of hawkweed is also remedial.

Dock leaf

Staphylococcus aureus has the ability to quickly acquire antimicrobial resistance, but the following herbal antibiotics can help cleanse the skin/follicle and begin to undermine the bacterial infection: thyme, goldenseal, red clover, spearmint, bee balm, mahonia and barberry.

Kitchen spa

Garlic juice used topically is antimicrobial, and eating some extra garlic or onion can detox the blood and skin. A poultice or compress of parsley can draw out the pus. Honey is the oldest antimicrobial agent, going back to those ancient Egyptians and the original plague of boils.

ECZEMA, PSORIASIS, DERMATITIS

Eczema, psoriasis and dermatitis are a group of conditions similar in many respects – they all cause dry, itchy, scaly skin – but each has different roots and is best treated differently.

Some garden herbs, such as chamomile and calendula, are good for all three. Chamomile is quite rich in sesquiterpene hydrocarbons, which work to calm skin irritations, and is also packed with azulene, which has anti-inflammatory and skin-healing properties. Heartsease is better for eczema, and green tea is good for allergic contact dermatitis. The tar (resin) of Scots pine was once used for psoriasis and eczema, but we can easily substitute that with the antiseptic essential oil of pine.

Heartsease

ECZEMA

Eczema is commonly first experienced in infancy and generally resolves between the ages of five and just before adolescence, but it can follow some people into adulthood. It is thought to be a reaction to environmental irritants or allergens and is not contagious. Avoiding harsh chemical and soap-based cleansers is essential to let the skin recover. Instead use healing herbs such as calendula, field scabious and chickweed to form the basis of home washes and soaps. The use of an emollient (either home-made or aqueous cream) infused with the same herbs will help maintain natural skin oils and also speed recovery.

Oatmeal and goat's milk mask

Soak ½ cup of oatmeal in 1 cup of goat's milk overnight. The next day mix with some sticky honey and apply the gloopy porridge to the affected area. Keep the excess to add to your bath. You can also strain the juice from the gloop to make a lotion.

Viola and calendula cream

Both viola and calendula have anti-itch and antihistamine properties. Simply soak the flowers overnight in full-fat cream, which is also soothing and nourishing to the skin. Next day use a mortar and pestle to mash a few tablespoons of the mixture and extract the full potency of the petals. Keeps for three days in the fridge. You can of course make a longer-lasting cream by infusing oil with the petals and mixing it with a petal tea and emulsifying wax, using any of the recipes in this book for lotions, creams or body butters.

PSORIASIS

Psoriasis is a chronic inflammatory, non-contagious skin disease. The condition accelerates the rate at which skin cells are produced, turned over and shed from a normal monthly cycle to a weekly one or even shorter. The fast turnover results in blotching, scaling and discomfort. The name is from the Greek word *psora*, meaning itch.

Most people develop psoriasis in their teens, early twenties or later in life after fifty. There are a few forms but the most common is known as plaque psoriasis, which manifests as distinctive patches of raised reddish skin covered with a whitish silver layer that eventually becomes scaly. Outbreaks are common on the elbows, knees, scalp and the lower back. Complications can include restricted joint motion; in fact the condition is in the same family as arthritis and about 10 per cent of cases go on to develop psoriatic arthritis.

Garden spa

A compress of steamed and cooled comfrey foliage is remedial to the itch. A lightly steamed cabbage compress is both soothing and antiseptic. Both evening primrose oil and borage oil are highly recommended for psoriasis. Use them in creams, lotions, salves or balms.

Kitchen spa

The oleic acid and omega 9 fatty acids in olive oil, if added to your diet, can suppress inflammation and treat flare-ups. Think also of foods that contain psoralen, a compound that supports the body's own defences to psoriasis and eczema. Psoralen-rich foods include figs, fennel, celery, celeriac, coriander, carrots, parsnips and parsley.

DERMATITIS

Dermatitis is literally the Greek for skin (*derma*) combined with the suffix used in medicine to denote inflammation (*-itis*). It takes many forms and has many triggers but the common denominators are an itchy rash or swollen, reddened skin that may blister or ooze, develop a crust and flake. Be it on the scalp, elbows, hands or body, there is help available to treat the inflammation.

Garden spa

Extracts of evening primrose oil and oolong tea or red peony tea can be drunk or used as a bathing solution. Aloe vera gel or strawberry pulp both cool and soothe flared-up skin. Make a salve from chickweed and calendula (see page 246), two excellent skin-healing agents, with some evening primrose oil for extra benefit and ongoing care.

Kitchen spa

Topical applications of coconut oil can, for many, reduce redness, dryness and scaling within a couple of days. Oatmeal is soothing and moisturising, as is honey. Apple cider vinegar is a non-steroidal anti-inflammatory that also helps resolve scaliness and itchiness.

Geranium, rose and chamomile body wash

For irritable skin conditions

Essential oil of pot geranium reduces inflammation of the skin and controls infection of wounds. Rose is a tonic and is soothing to skin, while chamomile is great with all complexion types and is gentle on seborrhoea and acne, while flushing toxins from skin capillaries.

Ingredients

- 500ml distilled/spring water
- 2 cups chamomile flowers
- 2 cups rose petals
- 1 cup geranium flowers and foliage
- 20g natural soap
- 10–15ml liquid soap (optional)
- 2 tablespoons vegetable glycerine

Geranium

Method

Decoct all the floral ingredients (see page 30 for instructions) and then strain to remove the solids. Bring back to the boil and grate in the solid natural soap. Simmer and stir until fully melted. Remove from the heat and allow to cool and set to a jelly (several hours). Now you can blitz it to break up the jelly into a runnier gloop. At this point you can add the liquid soap and glycerine. Finally decant into clean storage bottles. The froth bubbles will settle. Will store for up to one year, but it's generally used within months if not weeks of making.

SOME ESSENTIAL OILS AND THEIR SKIN BENEFITS

Clove: anti-inflammatory, antiseptic, antibacterial, antifungal, anti-infectious, analgesic, disinfectant.

Eucalyptus: antibacterial, antifungal, anti-infectious, anti-inflammatory, antiseptic.

Fennel: analgesic, anti-inflammatory, antispasmodic, antiseptic.

Geranium: anti-inflammatory, antibacterial, antifungal, antispasmodic, antiseptic, astringent.

Jasmine: antibacterial, skin tonic.

Lavender: antifungal, analgesic, antiseptic, anti-inflammatory, vasodilating.

Myrrh: antioxidant, anti-inflammatory, analgesic, anti-infectious, antiviral, antiseptic, astringent.

Pine oil: antiseptic, analgesic, energising.

Rose: anti-inflammatory, anti-infectious, relaxant, skin tonic, scar-reducing.

Rosemary: antifungal, antibacterial, antiviral.

Tea tree: antiseptic, antifungal, antiviral, antimicrobial.

Thyme: antiseptic, antifungal, antiviral, antimicrobial.

SCARS

Scars come in all shapes and sizes. Not all are easily resolved but with time most diminish somewhat. There are some helping hands available to speed up the natural process.

SHORT-TERM SCARS/MINOR SCARS

We all pick up cuts and burns in the kitchen, the garden, even getting ready to go out – a rushed shave or a curling-tongs mishap. These little accidents can leave scars. As part of the healing process they scab up. Messing with that scab causes more collagen to be sent to the site and it can stay after the wound has healed, leaving a longer-term scar. But most scars of a minor nature fade with time.

LONG-TERM SCARS

Even if you take care of a wound you may still end up with a scar, depending on the depth or severity of the burn or cut and the damage done to connective tissues. Wounds don't have to be deep to leave a scar; some people are simply more prone to scarring and some places, where skin is under tension, scar more easily.

SCAR TYPES

Flat scars. Minor-injury scars are generally pale and flat; most are temporary and fade back to your normal skin tone. Others do not fully fade and leave a more visible scar mark. Wound care is key to minimising these.

Raised scars (referred to as hypertrophic or keloid scars) are a result of the body producing too much collagen in response to the injury. Raised scars may flatten over a period of years. Topical applications of quercetin can help speed up the process.

Indented, or atrophic, scars are the pockmark scars often left behind after a bout of chickenpox or cystic acne. Because they result from damage to the underlying support structure, the skin cell or pore collapses in. Indented scars respond best to laser treatments and dermal fillers.

Garden spa

Many garden plants have properties that soften, fade or otherwise diminish scars. These are suitable for use in salves, lotions and washes. The trick is timing. You can treat before the scar forms or after it has formed. Below is advice on both.

REDUCING SCAR FORMATION

Topically applied infusions or salves of antibacterial herbs (thyme, chamomile, lavender, etc.) will help prevent wound infections and reduce the intensity of our natural repair response that produces scar tissue. Likewise, the anti-inflammatory treatments in this book can be used to treat wounds. Salves can keep the scar tissue moistened and help minimise it as it hardens into a permanent scar. Astringents that tighten wounds and promote skin-healing include witch hazel extract (see page 55) and St John's wort tea/oil.

DIMINISHING SCAR APPEARANCE

The sap of aloe, apart from being a soothing substance, has an enzymatic activity that can help reduce/eliminate scars. Use it as a moisturising gel, in body masks and in scrubs. Quercetin is found in dock leaves, corn poppy leaves, lovage and ginkgo.

Kitchen spa, to minimise scar formation

Aloe sap or a raw grated-potato poultice are beneficial in minimising burn scars. For cuts and nicks, try an antiseptic thyme infusion or a yarrow compress. A rub of fresh calendula flowers or a premade salve stimulates a faster healing response too. Botanical antiseptics you can use in a salve or a tincture include chickweed, echinacea, elderflower, goldenseal, lavender, thyme and sage.

Yarrow

Kitchen spa to diminish scar appearance

Fruit masks exfoliate the top layers of skin, diminishing the colour of scars through cellular regeneration. Topically applied quercetin can lessen appearance of the scar. It can be found in apple skin and flesh, grape skin, seeds and flesh, strawberries and green tea.

Essential scar tissue treatment

Essential oil of angelica is an excellent healer of wounds and scars. It can be added to honey to make a liquid plaster or, if you're using it on old scar tissue, it can be utilised in rubbing blends – for massaging – with avocado oil or coconut oil. Rose oil, frankincense and helichrysum oil are all very effective too.

STRETCH MARKS (STRIAE)

Stretch marks are irregular areas of skin – bands, stripes, or lines – which are usually the result of the rapid expansion of the skin (e.g. a growth spurt, weight gain, bodybuilding, pregnancy). Sometimes there is a hormonal link. Stretch marks can arise anywhere on the body but generally manifest in places where fat is stored such as the abdomen, thighs and buttocks, breasts, upper arms and underarms. They make their first appearance as red or purple lines but fade to silver-pink or sometimes white over the course of a few years. People with darker skin are less prone to stretch marks.

The medical name for stretch marks is striae, but be it striae distensae (linear depressions), striae atrophicans (symmetric marks), striae gravidarum (circular marks), striae rubra (red marks) or striae alba (white marks) they are all the result of tearing in the dermis triggered by skin expansion and not having enough collagen to fill the gap. The stretch band loses elasticity – the elastin snaps – and the site discolours and becomes a sort of scar tissue. The treatments for scar tissue on page 216 can reduce the visibility of striae. Some stretch marks resolve somewhat over time; others diminish but do not return to normal skin. Topical applications of vitamins A, E and C can improve colour and texture, helping to make them less visible.

Note: Commercial or home-made topical treatments will not make the indentations level with the surrounding skin or unsnap elastin fibres. They may, however, help with colour and texture. The aim is to diminish rather than to eliminate.

Garden spa

Calendula oil mixed with a crushed vitamin C tablet will deliver the skin-healing vitamins A, E and C. Grow your own veg. Homegrown veg often contains more alpha-lipoic acid than supermarket varieties. See *Kitchen spa* below to discover why that's so good for you. Mullein oil encourages elastin integrity and function and can be used topically to prevent stretch marks and also to treat scars. A poultice of comfrey leaves or comfrey-infused oil can help rejuvenate damaged skin. Beyond its wound-healing ability, it also improves skin's natural moisture-retaining properties and boosts inherent elasticity. It contains a compound known as allantoin that promotes skin-cell regeneration. By stimulating the growth of new cells it will diminish older, damaged cells but it may also help damaged or problem-prone skin to become more resilient.

Kitchen spa

Skin masks made with pulped fruits deliver alpha-hydroxy acid, which gently removes a top layer of skin cells above the marks and encourages healthier skin cells to grow beneath. Most culinary oils contain ample vitamin E, which is beneficial in diminishing stretch marks. Salt-, sugar- and coffee-based body scrubs can stimulate cell turnover and improve the texture of skin while lightening colour. Alpha-lipoic acid (present in commonly eaten foods and in supplements – see page 136) plays a role in stimulating our DNA to replicate Ribonucleic acid and also has the ability to switch off ongoing cellular damage, especially to collagen, improving the appearance of wrinkles and stretch marks.

THE MORE MATURE GARDENER

The more mature gardener, well established and a dab hand at every task, has braved the elements, stood against wind and gale, sleet and snow, laboured under hot sun and weathered drizzle and monsoon all to create a patch of paradise. But that same weathering may be showing or on the cusp of showing. Also, as we age the epidermis, or outer skin layer, gradually thins, often leading to a greying of the complexion or more visible blemishes. Our melanocytes (those pigment-containing cells) also begin to decrease in number but visibly increase in size – hence age spots. And all the while depletion and alterations in underlying connective tissue affect the skin's elasticity. At the extreme end, elastosis produces that leathery, weather-beaten appearance, once almost an occupational hazard, conspicuous in farmers, sailors, mountaineers, frontiersmen and other outdoor types; and yes, that includes us gardeners!

AGEING SKIN

Ageing skin has four main problems: loss of elasticity (sagging), wrinkles, complexion changes and age spots. Gardeners may have to contend with the possibility of a weather-beaten complexion but we are lucky in having natural daylight regularly reset or maintain our circadian rhythm and improve the quality of our sleep, which in turn lets the body, mind, spirit and also hair, nails, eyes and skin rejuvenate without depleting our nutritional reserves. So if we grow and eat our five a day, our antioxidant levels are also topped up to fight premature ageing. All that is left is to protect ourselves from sun damage, drying breezes and the battering rain. We should cover up where we can and rehydrate or pamper our skin and selves after such episodes.

Conquer ageing extract

Horse chestnut extract inhibits the ageing enzymes of elastase and hyaluronidase, which deplete collagen and elastin. Commercially produced extracts from the local pharmacy can be taken internally, but home-made extract can be used topically to remedy age blemishes, wrinkles, sagging skin and complexion issues. Conkers (as we call the nuts in Ireland) can be shelled and blended with other pro-collagen and pro-elastin herbs (mullein, rosemary, thyme, milk thistle and others mentioned throughout this book) and vitamin C to make oils, creams, lotions, bath blends and topical pastes.

SAGGING SKIN

We know that two types of protein – collagen and elastin – work in unison with oil-secreting glands in our skin to keep it plumped and replenished. As we age, protein depletions and alterations in underlying connective tissue affect the skin's elasticity – its tightness and ability to spring back – thus sagging occurs. Dehydrated skin is also an issue as we age, contributing to loss of plumpness and elasticity.

There is the theory of minimisation to consider: feed the skin with nourishing oils to lessen its need to deplete its own natural oil reserves, and also consume heart-healthy fats and oils to replenish stocks from within. The aim is to keep skin rejuvenated and maintain its firmness and elasticity longer.

Garden spa

Horse chestnut extract naturally conditions your skin by improving the circulation of oxygen-rich blood to the dermal layers, but it also firms it by inhibiting two skin-sagging enzymes – hyaluronidase and elastase – that deplete our reserves of collagen and elastin. Mullein oil provides astringent tannins and useful levels of elastin. Simply bathing with hops can be helpful, as it inhibits elastase. Borage oil and evening primrose oil are great topically and as supplements, but massage oils made by infusing calendula, nasturtium, peony and red clover can support natural tautness. Goldenrod baths have a history of use to tone flabby skin.

Kitchen spa

Diet is important and topical skin treatments with nutrients that support collagen and healthy skin (including vitamins A, E and C) are helpful. Omega 3 fatty acids nourish skin cells and are especially good at plumping and tightening skin from within (i.e. taken in your diet) or topically applied. As well as omega 3, nuts, legumes and oily fish are great sources of two trace minerals significant to wrinkle reduction: selenium and copper. Selenium is an antioxidant and so neutralises free radicals, but it also has a role in maintaining and restoring the skin's elasticity. Copper is essential to the production of both elastin and collagen. Soya-based foods may improve collagen levels.

Firming skin cream

Ingredients

- 6 tablespoons grapeseed oil (already sun-infused with borage and mullein flowers for two weeks)
- 1 tablespoon grated beeswax
- 1 tablespoon grated/granulated emulsifying wax
- 6 tablespoons witch hazel extract

Method

Warm the oil in a bain-marie and add the waxes. Keep the heat on until the waxes are fully melted. Remove from the heat and slowly add the witch hazel, whisking as you go. Allow to cool for 20 minutes and whisk again to a final creamy consistency.

BODY PAMPERING

MOISTURISING

The prime function of a moisturiser is to create a barrier film upon your skin's surface in order to prevent moisture loss. But in doing this, the moisturiser also hydrates dry skin and protects skin cells from damage. The home-made moisturisers in this book also feed our skin some key nutrients. Any of the skin tonic herbs can be made into a night cream or a body lotion, or for that extra luxuriant pampering, a body butter.

Luxurious manifold rose and honey body butter

Ingredients

- 1 cup coconut oil
- 1 cup raw/solid shea butter
- ½ cup rose-infused almond oil*
- 1 tablespoon honey

Method

In a bain-marie melt together the coconut oil and shea butter. Remove from the heat and fold in the almond oil and honey. Cool for 20 minutes before whisking the mixture till you achieve meringue-like peaks. Chilling in the fridge for 20 minutes at this point will help you get a creamier, thicker butter. An electric whisk will give the best results. Decant into a clean storage container.

The end product stores in the fridge or a cool bathroom for three weeks.

* To infuse almond oil, simply submerge as many rose petals as will fit into the bottle of oil and leave it by a sunny window for one to two weeks. If you can't wait that long, just add 10 shakes of essential rose oil at the whisking stage.

TONING

Your body's skin can also be toned. Witch hazel wipes, herbal vinegar spritzes and astringent body masks or body gels all work well.

Toning body jelly

In a small saucepan, boil ⅓ cup of water and ⅓ cup of pith of citrus fruit to release the pectin. Blitz in a blender and then strain off the lumpier bits. Add ½ cup of puréed aloe vera sap and 2 tablespoons of vegetable glycerine or honey. Stir well. Apply to the body and leave on for 15 minutes. Rinse off. Stores in the fridge for four days.

EXFOLIATION

As a gardener I am aware that the etymology of the word *exfoliate* (from the Latin *exfoliare*) comes from a description of a garden practice: to strip off leaves. It is interesting to think that many garden leaves and plants can strip off the dead skin cells adhering to our skin and diminishing our radiance. And that's what exfoliation does – it removes the dead skin that is slow to shed naturally, in a very helpful and usually gentle way. It's a helping hand from nature to refresh our skin. We often think of it as a facial process but the whole body is covered in skin, so it's okay to exfoliate as a treatment as well as a beautifier. Removing dead cells is beneficial to moving on pimples, acne, boils, blemishes, etc. It's turning over the soil, as it were, for fresh growth. Exfoliation also helps moisturisers and other skincare treatments penetrate the skin more effectively.

BODY EXFOLIANTS/BODY SCRUBS

Body scrubs not only slough off dead skin cells; the action of applying them actually boosts circulation to all layers of the skin, helping to eliminate toxins too. This combination action leaves skin supple and radiant. The dried rind of fruits, kitchen grains and many garden seeds and fruit seeds can be used to add a bit of extra roughage to home-made creams. Lotions, salves or gels can be modified to become exfoliants. Poppy or nigella seeds in a little aloe vera sap make ideal exfoliants. For the shower, the same ingredients with a little castile soap added provide an exfoliating body wash. These are for the body so be careful with the face and eyes.

How to make an exfoliant

As a general starting point, the ratio is generally 1:1 – equal parts wet to dry ingredients, be that 1 cup or 1 tablespoon. The wet agent can be a favourite oil, aloe vera gel or fruit juice. You can add extra wet or extra dry to achieve a consistency you prefer. It's okay to add a few drops of essential oil for extra tonic value and fragrance.

NATURAL EXFOLIANTS

A list of ingredients you can use in home-made exfoliants:

ALPHA-HYDROXY ACIDS (AHAs). The active ingredient used in chemical peels is present in many fruits but in concentrations that will not cause redness or inflammation. Add them to exfoliator mixtures and they ease the surface layers into shedding.

APPLES AND APPLE CIDER VINEGAR contain AHAs and other gentle acids that lift off dead skin cells. They also have value as a skin tonic.

BAKING SODA, BREAD SODA AND BICARBONATE OF SODA are all the same thing: sodium hydrogen carbonate. Many spa and clinical microdermabrasion treatments contain sodium bicarbonate. It's great for soothing the skin during exfoliation.

BETA-HYDROXY ACID (BHA). The stronger cousins of AHAs. Salicylic acid is a BHA.

CITRIC ACID is an AHA used in chemical peels and over-the-counter creams such as pH-adjusting agents. It is naturally found in citrus fruit juices and their pulp, rind and peel. Pharmacy supplies are best utilised in small quantities.

COFFEE. Caffeine stimulates cell turnover and increases blood circulation.

FRUIT. Fruit fibres and fruit seeds exfoliate. The fruit acids detach the surface dead cells revealing the new cells below, while the seeds slough off the dead cells. Try kiwi, strawberry, raspberry, cranberry or grape.

GLYCOLIC ACID is an AHA naturally sourced from sugar canes and sugar beets, grapes, pineapple and cantaloupe. It reacts with the surface of the epidermis to weaken the lipid bonds that bind dead skin cells together. This is not the version used in the textile industry, which is synthesised from formaldehyde.

HONEY makes a great base for an exfoliator as it is a humectant and a moisturiser with antiseptic, antibacterial, antiviral and antifungal properties, useful in reducing post-exfoliation inflammation.

HORSETAIL is somewhat abrasive, but because of its high silica content, it is often used to strengthen connective tissue and stimulate the production of new skin cells. It is an astringent and also has clarifying properties.

JUICE. Either use fruit juices that contain AHAs or the juice of aloe and houseleek, which make viscous gels that can be mixed with seeds or other ingredients in this list.

KEFIR contains lactic acid and is antibacterial and soothing. Mix with seeds, beach sand or coarse natural fibres for extra sloughing action.

LACTIC ACID is found in milk. It is more intense and cosmetically beneficial in soured milk products such as yoghurt, kefir, etc. It not only eases away dead cells through its keratolytic action (causing skin cells to loosen and shed) but also adjusts acidity and has nourishing properties.

LAVENDER FLOWERS (dried) can be added to a mixture of equal parts sugar or salt and olive oil to make a fragrant and skin-rejuvenating scrub.

LOOFAH. This is often thought off as an implement but it is actually a very natural product – a dried cousin of the cucumber that fruits on tropical and subtropical vines of *Luffa aegyptiaca* or *Luffa acutangula*. The coarse fibres easily slough off dead cells.

MILK. Use full-fat cow's milk for its lactic acid, which lifts older skin cells to reveal newer ones. A milk mix is great too – try some goats' milk to nourish, soya for softening, almond for suppleness or coconut for extra moisturising.

NUT FLOUR is a useful base in home exfoliants as both a sloughing agent and a thickener. It also contains skin-toning phytochemicals. Almond flour, for example, is soothing and contains mandelic acid, a prime component of many chemical face peels.

OATMEAL mixed with a little honey or milk is very effective at removing dead cells.

PAPAYA contains the enzyme papain, which actively dissolves dead skin cells, promotes resurfacing and fades age spots and blemishes in one fell swoop. Almost-ripe papaya contains more papain than ripe, so buy it when it's green.

PINEAPPLE contains papain and also bromelain, two enzymes that encourage cellular repair and naturally dissolve the bonds of dead skin cells.

PUMICE is a soft but abrasive volcanic rock. It's excellent for hard heels but it can be ground to 'sand' and used in exfoliation blends of oil or liquid soap.

RICE BRAN can be used as a dry exfoliant (boost it with some sugar if you like).

SALICYLIC ACID is a beta-hydroxy acid that can be sourced from willow leaves and bark. The acidity works as a dissolving agent on dead cells but it also opens clogged pores and neutralises bacteria.

SALT is a gentle abrasive but it also contains traces of calcium, magnesium, bromide and potassium, which promote healthy skin.

SEEDS. The grit to the slough can be sourced from leftover garden seeds or health-shop staples such as chia, flax, hemp, etc. Garden-sourced borage, sunflower and evening primrose will bring skin-healing properties too.

SUGAR. Sugar is a gentle abrasive but it is also a natural source of glycolic acid breaking the bonds with dead skin cells and promoting rejuvenation beneath.

TEA. Green and black tea are replenishing to skin and naturally loosen debris and dead cells.

VANILLA. To make something luxurious you can use vanilla-bean seeds. The fragrance is an aphrodisiac to butterflies, so don't stand near a buddleia bush for a day or so!

WILLOW (SEE ALSO *SALICYLIC ACID*). Willow water (soak some willow in water for a minimum of one week) can be used to mix with oatmeal, etc., as a keratolytic agent to be used on warts. The dried bark and foliage can also be used in mixes to provide some traction to the exfoliator.

YOGHURT contains lactic acid, but while it exfoliates it also hydrates and promotes smoother skin.

BODY AND BATH

The oldest beauty treatment in the world is bathing. The ancient Egyptians elevated bathing to legend even before Cleopatra glamorised it. The Romans made bathing into an art form and used it as a civilising practice (good enough to turn Attila the Hun). The Japanese brought it higher still. The Greeks may have begun the first spa treatments with their *balaneia* (public baths) and *spa* is a term originally used to describe a mineral-water bath cure. Even the Irish hero Cú Chulainn, when he wasn't bathing in blood or using seven vats of cold water to calm his boiling blood, took a dip in pleasant streams to revive himself, long before he met the invulnerable tide.

NATURAL BATH ADDITIVES

Some heal skin, some relax muscles and tissues, some relax your mind or raise your spirits. Why go commercial, which is mostly artificial fragrance and chemicals, when a bit of real nature can get you naturally beautiful?

ALFALFA. Traditionally used to diminish the pain and inflammation of arthritis and rheumatism. It will also help relieve general fatigue and muscle tenderness. It is a tonic to skin too.

APPLE CIDER VINEGAR is antifungal, antibacterial and is also a natural skin detoxifier. But best of all it helps alkalise your body's pH, prompting cleaner, clearer, more radiant skin.

ASSES' MILK. I dare you. In all seriousness, see *Milk* in *Natural exfoliants* on page 228.

BIRCH LEAVES are not only a disinfectant but their astringency can also benefit a variety of skin complaints from sunburn to cellulite.

BEER is not just good for hair and bad for pesky slugs, it can also help with psoriasis and inflamed skin. Just add a few bottles or cans to the bath and fill as normal.

CHAMOMILE has somewhat sedative properties as well as its skin-healing potential. It will deliver a bath that is refreshing to the body and relaxing to the mind. Great for dry or irritated skin.

EPSOM SALTS take their name from a saline spring in Epsom in England, where spas were popular during Roman times. In essence the salts are magnesium sulphate – a compound of magnesium, sulphur and oxygen, three great skin rejuvenators.

ESSENTIAL OILS are not just for fragrance but are also great skin-healing agents. See *Some essential oils and their skin benefits* on page 213.

FOLIAGE. All those mind-calming and body-toning herbs with skin-healing and anti-inflammatory properties can be added to the bath in muslin bags to benefit your skin and your olfactory senses. Remember, too, the trees – elder is great for skin, birch is cleansing, linden is toning and sedative.

GINGER is an anti-inflammatory and a natural skin detoxifier, extracting and flushing toxins from your body. Add 3 tablespoons of chopped fresh ginger to your bath oil, liquid soap or directly into the hot water.

GLYCERINE is an emollient and a humectant, so it's great for making bath oils or just adding directly to baths. Don't confuse it with nitroglycerin; we can keep that for pest control and new plant holes.

GREEN TEA is energising, anti-ageing and it's an antioxidant. What more do you need to know?

HOPS are nourishing and anti-inflammatory. They are brilliant for treating dry and environmentally stressed skin, but they also inhibit elastase, the enzyme that contributes to the ageing and sagging of skin.

HONEY is full of glucose oxidase, the agent that disinfects and heals wounds, treats skin inflammation and gently removes dead skin cells, etc.

JUNIPER BERRIES not only help to disinfect wounds, combat acne and address cellulite, they also smell wonderful. Throw a few sloes in and have a gin soak!

LAVENDER is not just fragrant, it is also adaptogenic: if you're down or tired, it picks you up, but if you're stressed or manic, it calms you down. It is soothing to skin and remedial to at least half the conditions in this book. It's almost a one-stop shop for skin health and personal well-being.

MELALEUCA (TEA TREE OIL) is certainly in the top five natural antibacterial and disinfectant additives that will remedy cosmetic and medical skin issues from acne and abscesses to blisters, bruises, rashes, sunburn, fungal infections and red inflammations.

OATS soothe inflamed skin, dislodge dead cells, tone and moisturise. Place in a muslin bag or in the foot of an old stocking.

PEPPERMINT both cools and stimulates, refreshing and revitalising the skin, as well as the mind and spirit. It can help to tone skin and close pores, reduce inflammation and redness and also improve the skin's elasticity.

ROSEMARY invigorates the body and mind. In a bath it is a useful astringent, antifungal, antibacterial and pore cleanser. Rosemary also stimulates blood circulation and elimination of toxins. It may help improve your skin's elasticity and appearance.

SAGE is uplifting and also calming. Best of all, its astringency works to treat oily skin and body acne.

SEA SALT. As little as 2 cups transforms your bath into a warm, welcoming ocean. Salty water has an ancient tradition in alleviating skin disorders and inflammation of muscles and tendons. It stimulates circulation, boosts the hydration potential of the water, boosts the action of essential oils, detoxes and promotes cellular regeneration.

SEAWEED makes an ideal detox bath. Its mineral content pulls toxins from your body, but its iodine and omega 3s nourish the pores and skin. Kelp and other seaweeds are loaded with iodine, magnesium, silica, calcium, potassium, phosphorus, iron and zinc. Rinse and add to your bath to soften and nourish skin. Seaweed also contains vitamins A, B, C, D, E, K and carotenes, so it can be blitzed with vegetable oil to extract the fat-soluble ones and then added as a bath oil.

SODIUM BICARBONATE (aka baking soda, bread soda and bicarbonate of soda) balances pH and tones skin.

TURMERIC is an antioxidant, an antiseptic and an anti-inflammatory, both when used in cooking and as a bath additive.

VOLCANO ASH. The product known as bentonite clay is essentially aged volcanic ash. The clay, or the ash, produces a sort of electrical charge when hydrated, which draws toxins from the skin, including heavy metals and residual chemicals.

WILLOW BRANCHES AND FOLIAGE are both packed with the pain-relieving 'natural aspirin' of salicylic acid (a BHA, see page 226). But it also softens skin, exfoliates dead cells, treats blemishes and fine lines and improves skin tone and texture.

YARROW is an astringent. It has wound-healing properties and also soothes irritation. It improves skin tone and texture and is beneficial to oily skin, acne, blemishes and skin tone.

The mother of all bath formulas

Ingredients

- 50ml green tea
- 50ml witch hazel extract
- 50ml horse chestnut gel
- 3 tablespoons apple cider vinegar with 'mother' in it (see page 140)
- 3 tablespoons sea salt
- 3 tablespoons Epsom salts
- 3 tablespoons glycerine
- 3 tablespoons honey
- 3 tablespoons dried ground ginger
- 3 tablespoons dried ground kelp
- 4 shakes of rose essential oil
- 150ml liquid soap

Method

Blitz all the ingredients in a blender and then decant into a clean storage bottle. Will keep for several weeks. Shake well before use.

HIPS, THIGHS
AND BUTTOCKS

Fat storage can be an issue, but how fat is stored can be a bigger problem. The conditions below can affect all three sites.

CELLULITE/ORANGE-PEEL SKIN

Cellulite manifests as a dimpled appearance on the skin, generally on the thighs, hips and buttocks. The problem arises within the fascia, or subcutaneous layer, of the skin. It is effectively an imbalance between the connective tissue and fat layer of skin, allowing fat to deposit in pockets left by collagen deficits, just below the surface of the skin. It is not necessarily an overweight issue, but poor diet and poor exercise can contribute. Thin women also develop cellulite. There may be some genetics at play, but there is also a hormonal element.

I have used the word *problem* in connection with cellulite, but the real problem is that society sees it as a problem. As many as 90 per cent of post-pubescent women develop cellulite. It is almost a secondary sex characteristic (men rarely get it). It's as natural as freckles and greying hair. In a way I feel we should just embrace it, love it, live with it as part of who we are. As a man I might not need to worry about it, but as a man I have to say that it is no preclusion to sexual attraction. That said, if you feel less sexy with it, there are ways of diminishing it.

Garden spa

That 'weed' dandelion may just be a friend indeed. The leaf has significantly higher levels of vitamin C and double the calcium content of garden lettuce. Included in a salad, its benefits include treating cellulite, arthritis and rheumatism.

Kitchen spa

Ditch the junk and processed food, bin the bad fats and eat a healthy diet rich in fruits, vegetables and plenty of fibre. Caffeine is the great stimulant of our day, but coffee is great for the skin – not drinking it but rubbing it into the skin to boost circulation. A little saffron hits two positive notes: it increases circulation and it inhibits expansion of fat cells. Apple cider vinegar, be it a spoonful taken direct, in a little apple juice or in a home-made salad dressing, delivers potassium, magnesium and calcium to relieve any water retention that shows up cellulite. It is also brilliant at flushing out toxins, including stress hormones, and as an agent to balance oestrogen production – all key factors in minimising cellulite formation.

Coffee scrub

Keep the used coffee from a percolator or a cafetière in a muslin bag or in the foot of an old pair of tights and use as a caffeine-releasing cleansing scrub. Or you can make a scrub with powdered coffee and honey. Add a touch of witch hazel or hot water to start releasing the caffeine before you add the viscous honey.

Grinning monkey coffee and orange skin lotion

Stimulating and detoxifying

The word *coconut* originally comes from sailor slang meaning grinning monkey, and you'll be grinning like one too when you feel the consistency of this lotion and see how it retextures your skin.

Ingredients

- 150ml black coffee
- 150ml orange-peel-infused carrier oil
- 90g coconut oil
- 30g emulsifying wax
- 30g cocoa butter or shea butter
- 5 shakes of orange or mandarin essential oil (optional)

Method

Make a cup of black coffee. In a small saucepan, heat and melt the oils (but not the essential oil), wax and butter. Once the wax has fully melted, remove from the heat and add the coffee and the essential oil (if using). Whip for 3 minutes and then refrigerate for 10 minutes, then whip again until you achieve a lotion consistency. Keeps in the fridge for several weeks.

CHICKEN SKIN

That bumpy chicken skin is an inflammatory condition known as keratosis pilaris. The problem is that skin cells have not just clogged the pore, causing inflammation, but that they have actually become hardened inside the pore. It is seen as a genetic issue and there is no cure as such, but reducing the inflammation and unclogging the pores will make a significant difference to appearance and texture.

Garden aid

Willow baths and anti-inflammatory teas will help. Teas can make great skin rinses, lotions or balms. Try basil, chamomile and rosemary.

Kitchen aid

Use a fruit exfoliate to gently lift away dead cells and open pores. Don't use a pumice or an abrasive scrub; scrubbing will only cause further inflammation. Add some anti-inflammatory foods to your diet. Beyond fish, there is omega 3 in seeds and nuts. Richly pigmented fruits and veg are also full of antioxidants. Get the fat balance right with avocados and olive oil (to provide monounsaturated fats). Cook with anti-inflammatory herbs and spices such as rosemary, parsley, basil, turmeric, ginger, garlic, celery seed and cardamom.

Salt and cracked black pepper body scrub

When eaten, black pepper can inhibit NF-kappaB, COX-1 and COX-2 enzymes, the agents of our body's inflammatory response. Used externally it can stimulate growth of new skin cells and exfoliate dead ones. Salt will also exfoliate. Simply mix 1 tablespoon each of salt and pepper in olive oil and massage well.

ARMS, HANDS
AND FINGERNAILS

ARMS

We are often exposed to the elements, with sleeves rolled up, and up to our knees if not our necks in weeding and other gardening chores, sometimes literally up to our elbows in compost. So it's no wonder that skin conditions are a perennial problem for gardeners. Arms are often on the front line.

Rosehip and sea buckthorn vit-arm-in potion

Topically applied vitamin C can protect the skin from UV and free-radical damage but it also plays a role in the synthesis of elastic fibres and collagen production to delay sagging arms and ageing skin. Two potent vitamin C sources from the garden are the berries of the sea buckthorn and rosehips.

Method

Simply blitz the hips and berries in equal quantities in a blender with enough buttermilk to cover. Strain through a muslin cloth and use the juice as a rub-in revitalising and photo-protective treatment.

ROUGH ELBOWS

To treat rough elbows just take half a lemon and use your elbow as a juicer. The juice and the action of the fruit flesh will soften them. Keep the juice to make a soothing emollient later (see the lotion below or any of the moisturising creams/treatments in this book). A poultice of the flesh of a fresh fig is not only tongue twisting but it softens rough elbows and hard heels too.

Echinacea and chickweed toning arm and elsewhere lotion

Chickweed

Topically, echinacea supports tautness and elasticity in skin and it is anti-inflammatory to overworked arm muscles. Chickweed not only supports the skin's natural cellular rejuvenation but is also remedial to blemishes and skin reactions. Suitable also for legs and décolletage.

Method

This has two parts to it.

To infuse an oil. To half a bottle or jar of carrier oil (sunflower, olive, argan, etc.) add as much chickweed and echinacea (flowers, foliage, crushed root) as will fit in the jar fully submerged. Add extra oil if required. Then sit the bottle/jar in a sunny window for two weeks or heat the bottle daily for one week in a pot of hot but not boiling water. When the herbs have infused, the oil may change colour and the plant parts will have lost some of their colour. You are ready now to make the lotion.

To make a lotion. In a bain-marie, simply heat 1 cup of the infused oil with ½ cup of emulsifying wax grains. Water is needed to mix with the oil to make the lotion. I like to make a cup of chickweed tea at this point rather than just add tap water, but you could also consider adding rose water, witch hazel, etc. Remove the wax-and-oil mixture from the heat and pour in ½ cup of water or tea. Stir well and then refrigerate for 10 minutes. Remove from the fridge and stir well again. If it is a little lumpy, you can whip with an electric whisk at this point. Will keep in the fridge for two weeks.

UNDER ARM

Natural deodorant

This is the tricky one as we are so conditioned to believe in the efficacy of sprays and roll-ons. Rose pastes or hydrosols are not only fragrant but also antibacterial. A deodorising lotion can be made using mint, lemongrass, geranium and other pleasing fragrances that also kill off the odour-triggering skin bacteria. A base of zinc ointment is antibacterial and odour-neutralising but it can stain. Sodium bicarbonate not only neutralises odour but also helps absorb moisture. Some like to dust it on but I have found it works great as a spray/spritz mixed with witch hazel or a floral hydrosol. There are many alternative commercial products that have less harmful stuff in them.

Natural antiperspirant

There are none that come close to modern expectations. Only chemical or mineral salts with aluminium traces can inhibit sweat glands. But the good news is that you can lessen your perspiration through diet changes. Vitamin C and foods rich in B vitamins actively encourage the elimination of excess toxins through your urine rather than via perspiration. Sage reduces the activity of the sweat glands. Fruits and veg with a high water content reduce body temperature, as does drinking water or iced teas. Normal tea is full of astringent tannic acid, which also inhibits odour.

HANDS

As gardeners our hands are casualties daily. The first line of defence is a good pair of gardening gloves. They don't have to be traditional gardeners' gloves; latex or surgical gloves work just as well and keep fingers more nimble for those tricky jobs when the gloves very often must come off.

HARD HANDS/WORK-ROUGHENED HANDS

Work-roughened hands benefit from light exfoliation. Simply pour 1 tablespoon or so of sunflower or olive oil into the palm of one hand and add 1 tablespoon of granulated sugar or sea salt. Then gently rub your hands together. The oil lubricates the gentle abrasion of the sugar or salt but its moisture penetrates simultaneously. Wipe off any excess oil with a towel.

Garden spa

For a more intensive exfoliating moisturiser, use a petal-infused oil (ox-eye, borage or calendula) with some sea salt and nigella seeds. Herbal balms are also helpful to rehydrate after a day's wear and tear. Soapwort is anti-inflammatory and cleanses the skin. The flowers of hedge privet soften and replenish skin.

Kitchen spa

Mix equal parts honey and lemon juice and massage into hard skin. You can also rub cider vinegar diluted with 7 parts water to 1 part vinegar into hard skin. Make a lotion from coconut milk and either honey or glycerine, adding the ingredients until you reach a suitable consistency.

Soapwort skin softener

The saponins in soapwort root provide the suds that earn it its common name and its reputation as a cleanser. This is good for all skin types. It is more the saponins than the actual suds that make water and skin softer.

Soapwort

Method

Simply boil up the root in water and use the liquid as a rinse, or add some gratings from a bar of natural soap to boost its lather potential. I like to bring to a boil and then simmer 20g of soapwort root in 400ml of green tea (1 tablespoon of green tea to every 100ml of water) for 30 minutes. It can smell a bit potent during the cooking phase, but once cooled and strained, this stores well and smells much better. You can make it with any herbal tea to boost it or simply use tap water if you prefer.

CALLUSES

A callus is just a thickening or hardening of the skin at points of friction or pressure. One can develop calluses on the palm of the hand and the rim of the thumb but most often with gardening, calluses develop at the base of the fingers, at the grip point for garden implements. Calluses are a natural defence mechanism to repeated friction and if they do not impair dexterity or cause pain, there may not be a rush to treat. Let them do their job for a while at least.

Garden spa

Calluses can be softened with salicylic acid (willow, meadowsweet, etc.) and the top hard layer of dead skin can be pumiced or otherwise exfoliated away. A soothing salve of calendula and chickweed will soften the callus prior to a pumice treatment and it will be remedial after too.

Top tip

Soften the skin with a soapy soak and exfoliate hard skin with a pumice stone. Never pare or cut away calluses.

Calendula and chickweed salve

Ingredients

- 1 cup fresh or dried calendula flowers
- 1 cup fresh aerial parts of chickweed
- 1½ cups olive oil
- ¼ cup beeswax shavings (approximately 25g)

Method

Crush or chop the calendula flowers and chickweed to help release their active ingredients. Then place them into a glass jar and completely cover with the olive oil. Cover with a lid. Bring a pan of water to the boil, turn off the heat and stand the filled jar in the hot water. Allow it to sit for 30 minutes to begin infusing. After 30 minutes turn the heat on again and simmer for a further 2 hours, adding water to the pan as evaporation occurs. Then turn off the heat and allow the receptacle to sit in the water and continue infusing for a further 30 minutes. This method is a shortcut version of the two-weeks-in-the-sunny-window method of infusing.

Strain off the solids from the oil and decant into a clean bowl. Chip, shave or grate the beeswax into the infused oil and stir until it dissolves fully and you get a homogenous mixture (add gentle heat using the bain-marie if needed). Finally, decant the mixture into a storage container and allow to cool and solidify before sealing and storing for use. The average shelf life of a home-made salve is approximately one year.

CHAPPED HANDS

Chapped hands are a consequence of hard work or harsh weather. Sometimes overexposure to water as much as to dry soil/sand/compost can cause chapping.

Garden spa

Washing with an infusion of yarrow is soothing and remedial, while a decoction of fresh or dried ox-eye daisy flowers is traditionally used to wash chapped hands. A lotion of both of these blended with olive oil and shea butter makes an excellent hand moisturiser.

Kitchen spa

A milk rinse or a yoghurt hand mask will soothe and replenish. Good old olive oil is rehydrating and hypoallergenic. The vitamins A and E contained in olive oil and sunflower oil will help repair and renew damaged skin.

Banana and avocado hand mask

For intense conditioning

Blend ½ a banana with 2 tablespoons of avocado oil and 1 teaspoon of honey. A good tip is to coat the hands and then cover with surgical gloves. Relax for 30 minutes and then remove the gloves and rinse your hands with tepid water.

Ground elder and elderberry hand mask

Compresses of ground elder reduce inflammation in the skin, partially due to the topical delivery of vitamin C. Elderberries are also packed with vitamin C, and the anthocyanins present (which give them their purple-black shine) are a powerful antioxidant (more powerful, some argue, than vitamin C or even vitamin E). Blitz or mash up equal quantities of ground elder and elderberries (⅓ cup each) with 1 tablespoon of honey. Wear for 20–30 minutes and then rinse away. This may stain your hands, so don't do it before you go ring shopping!

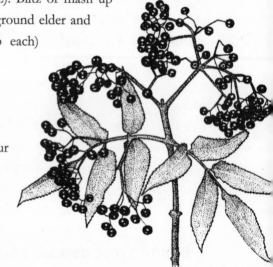

Elderberries

FINGERNAILS

Like the lawn, fingernails grow faster in summer. That said, they grow slowly enough, usually at a rate of 2–3mm per month. Diet and environmental temperature affect growth too. It generally takes your nails anywhere from three to six months to fully grow out – that's from cuticle to tip. So a blemish or indentation in the centre of the nail will be gone in a season.

Nails are in essence a type of modified skin composed predominantly of a substance called keratin, the same fibrous protein that makes up your hair. While we readily acknowledge hair as a living part of our body, sometimes we neglect the life in our nails. To maintain optimum nail health, what we feed them is as important as what we eat to keep our heart strong, skin radiant and hair lustrous.

MAXIMISING HEALTHY NAILS

Eat right. Asparagus, aubergines, celery and potatoes are good sources of zinc, which helps with nail integrity. Iodine in our diet helps keep nails tough. It doesn't have to be sushi and seaweed every night, though. It can also be a Saturday night saag aloo (spinach and potatoes), or indeed strawberries and hazelnuts on breakfast cereal. Calcium and iron also contribute significantly to nail health, and leafy veg, legumes and nuts will supply both of those.

SIGNS OF A POTENTIALLY SERIOUS PROBLEM

There is a whole range of nail inconsistencies, many down to a light trauma, some due to mineral deficiencies, but some, too, that indicate an underlying or emerging medical condition. Signs that should be seen by a medical professional include severe discolouration, dramatic curling or strong pitting of the nail, and of course any separation of the nail from the nail bed.

HOME MANICURE

Bleaching nails/tip whitener

To instantly go a shade lighter or to clean dirty nails, just steep in lemon juice to lift stains and bring up whiteness. Make a baking-soda finger bath with a little tepid water. You can regularly paint on a mixture of 1 tablespoon of lemon juice and 1 tablespoon of olive oil to lighten and moisturise simultaneously.

Cuticle softener

Paint on a mixture of 1 tablespoon of olive oil to 1 tablespoon of lemon or lime juice.

Honeyed jasmine cuticle balm

In a bain-marie, melt together 25g beeswax, 2 tablespoons of honey, 3 tablespoons of olive oil and 150ml of jasmine oil. Set in storage containers.

NAIL PROBLEMS

SOFT NAILS

Fragile nails can indicate rheumatism, poor diet or poor general health. Iron deficiency produces soft nails as does a lack of biotin (vitamin H) or zinc.

BRITTLE NAILS (onychoschizia and onychorrhexis)

Brittle nails occur in two directions: horizontal splitting is known as onychoschizia, while vertical splitting is called onychorrhexis. Women and older people are most affected by the syndrome. Age degrades keratin in the nail structure, as does the acetone in nail polish remover.

Garden spa

Use a mortar and pestle to crush some horsetail and paint on the extracted liquid, which is rich in nail-strengthening silica. Silica is also present in dandelions, asparagus, alfalfa, cabbage and cucumbers.

Kitchen spa

Biotin from avocados, mushrooms, Swiss chard and sunflower seeds will strengthen nails from within. Applied topically the natural oils from crushed sunflower seeds can also strengthen. An avocado hand mask will treat not just the nails but also the whole hand. For an internal top-up of silica, eat olives, oats, radishes, bell peppers, rice, millet and soybeans. The same ingredients work well topically too.

CRACKED NAILS

Cracked and split nails can beset gardeners as much as kitchen porters and it's the same basic cause in both cases – repeated exposure to water and substances (detergents or hot compost) that degrade the keratin that is responsible for the structural integrity of your nails. On average, healthy nails have around 15–18 per cent water content. Less than that leads to brittle nails that split and crack easily, but anything approaching 30 per cent water content also triggers cracking. Some of the bonds in the keratin glue dissolve at that degree of saturation and nails quickly soften and become damaged.

The answer is to moisturise your nails without saturating them. That can be as simple as an olive oil nail bath, and if you blitz some comfrey and horsetail in the oil base, the extra silicon and phytochemicals can strengthen as well as improve water-proofing.

HANGNAILS

Hangnails are those torn pieces of skin right at the edge of a nail, easily occasioned if you are a nail biter. Stop biting and don't worry – the dahlias will come up! Hangnails can also be caused by cold weather, immersion in water or by exposure to detergents and other harsh chemicals. Pamper your nails and use an antibacterial wash to prevent hangnails becoming complicated by infections such as paronychia.

RIDGES

Occasionally, raised lines develop in the nail. These are often a harmless, natural disruption to normal nail-growth patterns but are occasionally indicative of trauma or a medical condition. They can appear horizontally or vertically. Often they will simply grow out. Any nail nourishment, be it externally through a horsetail finger bath or internally through eating zinc-rich foods, etc., will benefit the condition of your nails.

BEAU LINES

Not quite a love letter, rather a condition of the nail matrix that occurs when cells temporarily stop dividing. Nail growth is a result of normal cell division; the renewal/production of new cells from the matrix simply pushes the older cells outwards towards the fingertips. The grooves run parallel to the base of the nail bed and are different from vertical ridges. Beau lines predominantly occur after/during illness or trauma, either trauma to the person or direct trauma to the nail such as a hammer blow. The shock of an early frost won't do it.

VERTICAL RIDGES

These are ridges running from the base of the nail to the tip. They are not generally occasioned by illness as with beau lines but rather occur (or increase in prominence) with age.

YELLOW NAILS

Tea, nicotine, turmeric and peaty soils can all stain nails. But talk to your GP to make sure it's not indicative of a medical condition. To whiten stained nails simply paint on a mixture of 1 tablespoon lemon juice to 1 tablespoon olive oil.

WHITE SPOTS/LEUKONYCHIA

These are commonly a result of minor trauma, not a vitamin deficiency as is often thought. The only effective treatment is to wait for the nail to grow out, slowly pushing the spot to the tip as the nail grows. Leukonychia can also manifest as white streaks. Sometimes an eczema outbreak can cause spotting on the nails, and some fungal infections begin as white spots, but neither are leukonychia. Fungal infections need treatment (see *Fungal nail infection* opposite). Persistent spotting may indicate a liver- or kidney-function issue and should be discussed with your doctor.

WHITE FLECKS

Flecking can indicate a zinc deficiency or just be the temporary 'scar' from a trauma to the nail fold (located just under the cuticle). As it grows out, it becomes visible. Eating cereal with milk a few times a week supplies zinc and other nutrients that help meet the deficit. Nuts and seeds also help.

PITTING

When small depressions develop upon or within the nail surface it can be an indication of an underlying medical condition. Pitting can lead to the nail loosening and even detachment from the nail bed. Psoriasis can cause pitting.

CURVING NAILS/KOILONYCHIA

Koilonychia is an abnormal growth pattern of the fingernail where the nail becomes thin, develops raised ridges and curves inward. It is an indication of an iron deficiency and often accompanies anaemia. Time to eat more brassicas and possibly take a supplement.

PEELING CUTICLES

The wear and tear of doing chores around the house and garden can damage the cuticle, and the overuse of nail polish and remover is another culprit here. Moisturising is key to cuticle health.

FUNGAL NAIL INFECTION/ONYCHOMYCOSIS

There are several fungi that can do damage to nails. Yeast such as *Candida albicans*, dermatophytes such as *Trichophyton rubrum* and even moulds in the *Fusarium* family can all infect the nails.

Fingernail infections respond quicker and more reliably than toenail infections to both home and pharmaceutical treatments. Many infections are deactivated by topical antifungals but some will require oral medication. Antifungal plants can be applied directly and some make nice teas that fight from within (thyme, sage, chamomile, etc.). Essential oils are antifungal by nature and tea tree is particularly effective.

Fungal infections can manifest in different ways:

- **Candida infection** develops first with an inflamed or red cuticle followed by white, yellow, green or black marks. The nail may loosen and lift.

- With **distal onycholysis** the tip of the nail lifts up and often the free edge crumbles.

- In **lateral onychomycosis** opaque white or yellow streaks appear along one side of the nail.

- **Proximal onychomycosis** manifests as yellow spots within the lunula (the half-moon).

- In **subungual hyperkeratosis** scaling occurs underneath the nail.

- Superficial **white onychomycosis** causes flaky white patches within the nail plate and often pitting too.

- **Tinea manuum** generally arises after injury and manifests as itchy scaling with redness.

LEGS, FEET
AND TOENAILS

LEGS

Some cultures think the ears are erogenous, others the nape of the neck and so on, but all agree that legs are something to behold. Looking after the load-bearing part of your body is important, but to make the most of those pins there are some things to be getting on with. (See page 86 for hair removal.)

Grinning monkey coconut and lime leg lotion

For soft skin
This moisturising lotion smells and feels great, and you'll be grinning like a monkey when you see how well it works.

Ingredients
- 150ml lime-leaf-infused carrier oil
- 90g coconut oil
- 30g cocoa butter or shea butter
- 30g emulsifying wax
- 150ml coconut milk/water
- 5 shakes of lime essential oil (optional)

Method

Heat and melt all the butter-, oil- and wax-based ingredients (except the essential oil) while you chill the coconut water/milk in the freezer. Once the wax is fully melted, remove from the heat and add the essential oil and chilled coconut water/milk. Whip for 3 minutes and then refrigerate for 10 minutes. Whip again to achieve the consistency of a lotion and keep refrigerated thereafter for longer storage.

Energising leg gel

In a blender, blitz equal amounts of mint leaves, coffee grounds and chopped aloe vera (⅓ cup) with 2 tablespoons of witch hazel and 2 tablespoons of glycerine. Stores in the fridge for one week.

Quick-fix leg-firming cream

Mullein is a firming herb and witch hazel will tighten. Make a decoction of the foliage by boiling it with the lid on for 20 minutes. Use 1 part herb to 3 parts witch hazel extract plus 1 teaspoon of oatmeal to every cup of water. Post boiling, cool fully and then sieve through a muslin cloth to remove the hairs and oatmeal gloop. Blend or whip the strained water with Silcock's Base or other emollient until at a consistency that works for you, or make as per the lotion method (see page 38) with 75 per cent oil and wax to 25 per cent fluid content.

LEG CONDITIONS

HIGH HEELS, LOW POINTS

If you're a gal who's constantly in heels, remember that they lead to varicose veins and premature foot wrinkling. Heels can tire your feet too, so any of the pampering treatments here will help.

HOT LEGS

While this is an invisible reaction/sensation and not a visible cosmetic issue, hot legs can contribute to restless nights and agitation during the day, which can cause frown lines and eye bags, so I think it's worth including this here.

Garden spa

Try a cooling menthol rub by gathering ½ cup of mint fresh from the garden and blitzing it in a blender with a drizzle of glycerine and ⅓ cup of carrier oil or green tea. Menthol selectively stimulates nerve endings that are sensitive to cold and so produces a sensation of coolness.

SWOLLEN LEGS (AND SWOLLEN ANKLES)

Swelling of the lower limbs can be a consequence of venous insufficiency, part of the menstrual cycle, pregnancy or just standing about too long or sitting down for extended periods. In the case of sitting or standing too long, the swelling is triggered by the retention of fluid, also known as peripheral oedema, a propensity for which can be a sign of a problem with the circulatory or lymphatic systems or of a kidney-related issue.

Garden spa

A dandelion diuretic does not deplete potassium and is a tonic to the kidneys. Use the leaf in a salad and the root in a beverage. Juniper berries and horsetail are also diuretic. Ginkgo, garlic and hawthorn will boost circulation and cleavers, pasque flowers and echinacea are tonics for the lymphatic system. Try the horse chestnut treatment on page 262.

Ginkgo

Kitchen spa

Cranberry juice and lemon juice are diuretics. Health-shop extracts of red vine leaf (grape leaf) can benefit microvascular blood flow and they oxygenate the blood too. The result is a natural anti-inflammatory. Grapes can support microvascular blood flow too, and having a Greek meal of *dolmadakia* (herbed rice wrapped in grape leaf) is a great way of getting those beneficial phytonutrients and also the antioxidant and anti-inflammatory omega 3.

Lymphatic tonic

In a blender, blitz 1 tablespoon of diuretic and fat-metabolising apple cider vinegar, 5 deseeded grapes to improve blood flow and to add some resveratrol, 1 stoned peach for its diuretic and detoxifying properties, ½ cup of cranberry juice, which helps towards amending any stubborn fat and shifts it from the lymphatic system, ½ cup of beetroot juice, which is diuretic and helps to get rid of fatty deposits, 1 tablespoon of parsley as a lymph detox and 1 tablespoon of honey as a sweetening anti-inflammatory.

VARICOSE VEINS

Be it a noticeable blue vein that has become more prominent or an outright bunch of grapes, varicose veins are the next step in venous insufficiency in the legs. Compression stockings work best but there is some good support too from the garden.

Garden aid

Internally hawthorn strengthens the capillaries. Horse chestnuts do the same, used both internally and externally. Horse chestnuts are rich in saponins; one in particular, called escin, is both anti-inflammatory and vasoprotective. Tinctures/extracts have a long history as oral medication to recirculate trapped deoxygenated blood from bruises, haemorrhages and varicose veins. Escin is most beneficial in strengthening the walls of capillaries, veins and arteries. It effectively diminishes the presence of elastase and hyaluronidase, two enzymes that break down protein and contribute to venous insufficiency and varicose veins.

Note: One reason for its effectiveness is that the extract also thins the blood by impairing the action of platelets.

Horse chestnut extract

Stimulates blood circulation and strengthens delicate blood vessels.

In autumn gather some chestnuts. Remove each nut from its spiny green case. Crack the shell and remove the meal. Place all the meal in a blender and cover completely with vodka. Blitz to a paste. Add more vodka if the consistency is too thick. Some herbalists like to let this extract sit for some weeks before siphoning off the liquid, but I find the blend holds well (shake if needed) in the fridge or a dark cupboard and becomes more potent and effective, especially for topical applications. Tinctures of horse chestnut for internal use can be made in the traditional tincture way or bought from health shops.

The extract can be applied topically in lotions, gels, creams or compresses.

Horse chestnut

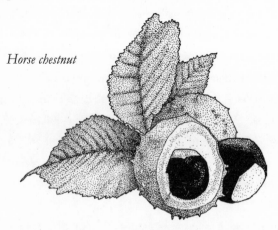

FEET

Gardener's feet are often as active as their hands, pacing drills, heeling in, providing pressure to the spade, locomotion to the wheelbarrow, and so on and on. But our feet are vital to our overall health and our overall health is vital to our overall appearance. So beyond the pedicure and the beautification of feet, paying attention to them may just show on our face, in our demeanour and even in the healthy lustre of our hair.

THE BENEFITS OF BAREFOOT GARDENING

When we walk the earth barefoot, be it on the sand of a beach, the soil of a field, a dew-soaked grassy hill, the forest floor or just the everyday lawn in our very own garden, a splendid magic happens. We connect with the earth, and it in turn, with every step, connects us to health and a natural realignment with the forces of life.

With each barefoot step, a multitude of free electrons from the earth's magnetic field will travel through the soles of your feet into your body and energise your living self. But this is no tingle or buzz that you might get from the static energy of a TV screen or a balloon rubbed on hair; there is nothing static here. There is transformation and there is movement. The fact is that these earth-gifted, negatively-charged free electrons are among the most potent antioxidants known to man. They can reduce inflammation, decrease our perception of pain, improve metabolism, alter the viscosity of blood, tone cardiac muscle, promote healthy sleep, pep up your sex life, even go a way to slow the signs of ageing and delay the progression of many chronic diseases.

Standing barefoot on your lawn for five minutes a day is a detox for your body that improves the function of your organs and skin. We age our bodies, dull our complexion, grey our hair and generally look haggard through the reaction of hydrogen peroxide in living tissue – that H_2O_2 which is naturally and constantly forming in our bodies. But standing barefoot increases the production and function of an enzyme called catalase, the role of which is to accelerate the decomposition of hydrogen peroxide back to simpler structures such as water (H_2O) and oxygen (O_2). So going barefoot can break down hydrogen peroxide before it breaks us down. Not such a weird idea now, is it?

HOME PEDICURE: PAMPER NIGHT

Tonic foot soak

To a basin, add 1 tablespoon of mustard powder, 1 tablespoon of Epsom salts, 500ml of warm water and 500ml of tonic water. Soak away. Pat dry when done and move on to exfoliating and moisturising.

Beach-feet exfoliant

Next time you're at the seaside or the tropical fish shop, why not get yourself ½ cup of beach sand? The minerals and the grittiness make it a great exfoliant when mixed with equal parts sea salt (you can buy it – no need to boil off the seawater!), olive oil and a few leaves of rosemary for extra stimulation.

Pep in the step moisturising lotion

Olive oil is deeply moisturising to skin and can be infused with the cooling and stimulating properties of peppermint (which also boosts circulation). Fill a jam jar ⅔ full with peppermint foliage (and any other mint leaves you may have) and cover with oil. Put the lid on the jar and sit it in a pot of boiling water for 20 minutes twice daily for three days, keeping it on a sunny window ledge between boils. Once infused, whip up a quick lotion by melting together ½ cup of the peppermint oil with 4 tablespoons of beeswax and 4 tablespoons of emulsifying wax in a bain-marie. In the meantime make a strong cup of peppermint tea. Add ½ cup of the tea to the oil-and-wax mixture. Whip with an electric whisk to achieve a creamy consistency. Keeps for several months.

Two-salts foot soak for swollen or tired feet

Add 3 tablespoons each of Epsom salts and sea salt to a basin of warm water. Epsom salts are really magnesium sulphate, which can reduce swelling and assist with the elimination of toxins from the body. Sea salt also draws toxins from the skin. Both salts cause a reduction in fluid retention. But beyond these benefits there is the bonus of thalassotherapy – a method of relaxation favoured by the Ancient Greeks that basically involved bathing in warmed seawater, *thalassa* being the Greek word for sea.

CORNS AND FOOT CALLUSES

Corns and calluses are localised areas of thickened skin. The main difference is pain. While a corn (clavus) is inflamed and painful, a callus (tyloma) is just plain old hard, dead skin and is painless. There are 'soft corns' (heloma molle) which seem to fall in between, generally arising where the skin is damp; pain might not occur but peeling and other complications can arise.

CORNS

Corns are identifiable by virtue of having a tip or a cone shape. Hard corns usually form on the tops or outer sides of the toes, just where the skin rubs against the shoe, hence the popularity of corn plasters. Soft corns generally form between toes at the point where the bones of one toe exert some pressure on the bones of the toe next to it. This is why it's important to wear shoes that fit. Corns are unsightly and beautiful feet can do without them.

CALLUSES

On hands or feet, calluses have no tip. They generally form over a flat surface; in the case of feet that means the weight-bearing parts (the ball or the heel). Calluses are part of our natural protection system; we develop them to protect the skin against chafing and pressure. Padding and insoles may be your best friends, but if it's a day for the sandals or a night for the heels, there are things that can be done.

Garden spa

Some work boots are just not cut out for maintaining soft and supple feet, so after a hard day at it, it's good to soften skin with a soapy soak (add a little Epsom salts or baking soda for extra relief) and then exfoliate any hard skin with a pumice stone. Never pare or cut away calluses or corns. You can treat corns and calluses on feet in the same way as recommended in the *Hands* section (see *Calluses* on page 245). Willow water is an excellent foot soak as it is softening, exfoliating and medicating. Mix with mint to provide a cooling sensation and extra soothing. The pulped nuts of the horse chestnut tree (or a premade extract) have great skin-softening properties, as does the sap of houseleeks.

Mallow and chamomile foot soak

Both mallow and chamomile contain mucilage that softens feet and phytonutrients that replenish the skin and address wounds and swelling. Make a decoction of ½ cup each per 1 litre water.

HARD/CRACKED HEELS

Our footwear can dry out our feet, and standing for long periods can undermine the efficiency of our sweat glands to naturally moisturise. Any of the moisturisers or fruit masks in this book will help here.

Garden spa

Horse chestnut extract has excellent skin-softening properties. A paste of the nuts (meal of nut blitzed with plain water or cider vinegar) can be applied topically. A willow footbath will help exfoliate dead cells. Traditional herbal emollients used to soften skin include plantain, chickweed, coltsfoot, elecampane, mallow and borage, all suitable for use in poultices, milk decoctions, footbaths, salves or oil infusions.

Kitchen spa

Mix equal parts honey and lemon juice and massage into hard skin, or make a cider vinegar rub using 7 parts water to 1 part vinegar. Use 1 tablespoon of sugar to 1 tablespoon of vegetable oil to make a fine scrub to slough off dead cells and rejuvenate skin. Simply rub into the feet, and after a pause to let the oil soak in and rehydrate skin, towel off any excess.

Sugar plum foot gel

Pulp a ripe plum with 2 tablespoons of dark sugar and massage into your heels. Apply some extra pulp and leave on for 10–15 minutes before rinsing, drying and applying a foot moisturiser.

Natural pumice foot scrub

Mix 1 tablespoon of witch hazel, 1 tablespoon of glycerine or honey and 1 tablespoon of poppy or nigella seeds with 3 tablespoons of puréed aloe sap and 3 tablespoons of coarse sea salt. Keeps for five days in the fridge.

TOENAILS

Toenails grow faster in summer than they do in winter; some argue that this is due to the change in seasonal footwear rather than the seasons themselves. Open-toe shoes and sandals allow more sunlight on the nails, increasing the actions of vitamins D and E and encouraging growth. There's a clue in that to which foods and topical treatments are good for healthy nails.

Top tip

Toenails are alive! They need to breathe to maintain optimum health. So constantly wearing nail varnish can undermine strength and also the ability to fight infection. Go nude as much as you can (and I don't say that too often).

TOENAIL PAMPER KIT

Cuticle oil

Sun-infuse (for two weeks) 3 tablespoons each of calendula petals, chopped horsetail leaf (or silica-rich borage leaf) and chopped rose or peony petals in 100ml of sunflower oil. This softens and nourishes cuticles and brings a sheen to nails.

Nailed it strengthening solution

Blend together 1 tablespoon of chopped comfrey root, 1 teaspoon of Epsom salts, 1 teaspoon of milk, 1 teaspoon of olive oil and 2 tablespoons of horsetail. Paint on nightly for a week. Keeps in the fridge for one week.

Bleaching juice

Lemon juice can whiten nails right up. Mix with a sprinkle of Epsom salts so as to add rather than subtract from the integrity of the keratin of the nail.

Snack attack

If after all the pampering you're a bit peckish, why not try sliced fig and peanut butter/brittle on toast, to boost your intake of minerals that support healthy nails?

TOENAIL PROBLEMS

INGROWN NAIL

Get it removed by a professional podiatrist.

MISSHAPEN NAILS/ ABNORMAL GROWTH

See *Fingernails* on page 255.

DISCOLOURED NAILS

Discoloured nails can indicate a health issue or simply be a result of a nutritional deficiency. Cosmetically, nail varnish can mask the underlying condition, but medical intervention will solve both symptom and cause.

Red: A defined redness can indicate hypertension.

Yellow: Yellow nails can be related to psoriasis or indicate a fungal infection, but sometimes they are due to a more serious medical condition. **Yellow nail syndrome** is not a fungal infection, but rather a symptom of lymphoedema (swelling of the legs and other body parts due to poor drainage of the lymphatic system) or of several lung complaints including pleural effusions and chronic bronchitis or serious sinus infections. It's a visit to the GP, not a pedicure, that's required here. Oral and topical vitamin E can be effective in controlling yellow nail syndrome and can help with lymphoedema too.

Blue/purple: Beyond a bruise on a stubbed toe, blue or purple can suggest circulatory problems.

Green: More than likely a candida infection.

Brown can also indicate a fungal infection.

Black: Beyond a bruise, this can also indicate a fungal infection. An infusion of thyme or an arnica tincture can remedy both issues.

White streaks or patches in the nail indicate a fungal infection.

Pale nails tend to indicate anaemia or a circulatory problem.

NAIL FUNGUS

Fungal infections often begin as a white or yellow spot or streaks on the surface or within the shell of the toenail. Once the fungus goes deeper, it will become more unsightly with crumbling edges. As the fungus lives and thrives beneath the nail it becomes more difficult to treat.

> ### Top tip
>
> Dig out the flip-flops or sandals and expose your toes to fresh air as often as possible. This will deprive fungus of the hot sweaty conditions in which it thrives.

Garden spa

Infusions of arnica, thyme or yarrow can not only reduce inflammation of the nail bed but also undermine the fungus. A chamomile paste made with mashed flowers and some tea tree oil is quite effective but requires daily application over several weeks. A footbath of chamomile and mint with 1 teaspoon of Epsom salts added is beneficial. Thyme is a very effective antifungal.

Kitchen spa

Soaking the toes in apple cider vinegar can help to destroy the fungus. Garlic juice is also an antifungal. Eating garlic will boost your immune system too. Zinc-rich foods not only increase immunity but, used topically, inhibit fungi. Try a poultice of spinach and wheatgerm oil or a paste of pumpkin seeds. Those soluble vitamin tablets or flu capsules that are full of vitamin C and zinc can be applied topically too. Simply crush and mix with a few drops of water to make a paste.

BRITTLE TOENAILS

Fragile nails can indicate rheumatism, poor diet or poor general health. Iron and biotin deficiencies both trigger brittle nails.

Garden spa

What we need to do here is grow iron-rich vegetables, but those dark kales and purple sprouting broccoli go well in an ornamental border too. You don't have to rip your garden up for a veg bed. Think potager!

Kitchen spa

Celery, asparagus and potatoes are rich and tasty sources of zinc. Iron is easily acquired from leafy green vegetables but also from legumes and nuts. The other benefit of legumes and nuts is that they supply nail-strengthening iodine and calcium.

GROOVES

Nails with grooves hint at a deficiency of vitamin B.

HANGNAILS

These are 'shards' of dry skin rather than flakes of nail. They are often a sign of vitamin deficiency. Moisturising helps prevent them from occurring.

INDEX OF PLANTS

INDEX OF RECIPES

GENERAL INDEX